50 BUILDINGS
YOU SHOULD KNOW

50 BUILDINGS
YOU SHOULD KNOW

Isabel Kuhl

Prestel
Munich · Berlin · London · New York

Front cover from top to bottom:
The Doge's Palace, Venice, from 1340
Jørn Utzon, Sydney Opera House, 1957-73
Günther Behnisch, Olympic Park Munich, 1968-72
The Great Pyramid of Giza, 2554-2531 BC
Frontispiece: William van Alen, Chrysler Building, New York, 1928-30
Pages 10/11: The Parthenon, Athens, 447-432 BC

Prestel Verlag
Königinstrasse 9
80539 Munich
Tel. +49 (89) 38 17 09-0
Fax +49 (89) 38 17 09-35

Prestel Publishing Ltd.
4 Bloomsbury Place
London WC1A 2QA
Tel. +44 (0) 20 7323-5004
Fax +44 (0) 20 7636-8004

Prestel Publishing
900 Broadway. Suite 603
New York, N.Y. 10003
Tel. +1 (212) 995-2720
Fax +1 (212) 995-2733

www.prestel.com

The Library of Congress Control Number: 2007929006

British Library Cataloguing-in-Publication Data: a catalogue record for this book is
available from the British Library. The Deutsche Bibliothek holds a record of this publication
in the Deutsche Nationalbibliografie; detailed bibliographical data can be found under:
http://dnb.ddb.de

Project management by Katharina Haderer, Claudia Stäuble
Translated from the German by Robert McInnes, Vienna
Copy-edited by Reegan Finger and Chris Murray, Crewe
Cover and design by LIQUID, Agentur für Gestaltung, Augsburg
Layout and production by zwischenschritt, Rainald Schwarz, Munich
Picture research by Andrea Weissenbach
Timeline and glossary by Edgar Kroll, Hamburg

Origination by Repro Ludwig, Zell am See
Printed and bound by Druckerei Uhl GmbH & Co. KG, Radolfzell

Printed in Germany on acid-free paper

ISBN 978-3-7913-3838-5

CONTENTS

2650–2150 BC OLD KINGDOM IN EGYPT (3RD–6TH DYNASTIES)

2639–2504 BC 4TH DYNASTY WITH THE PHARAOHS KHUFU
(CHEOPS), KHAFRA (CHEPHREN) AND MENKAURA (MYKERINOS)

FROM 2500 BC Development and peak
of the urban Indus Valley culture
(as many as 40,000 inhabitants)

ca. 2900 BC Graves with cord-ware ceramics in North
and Central Europe

ca. 2650 BC Construction of the first pyramid
(step pyramid of Djoser) in Saqqara

ca. 2750 BC Beginning of silkworm breeding in China

ca. 2420 Egyptians sail to
southern Africa

BRONZE AGE 3000 BC–1000 BC

| 3000 BC | 2965 | 2930 | 2895 | 2860 | 2825 | 2790 | 2755 | 2720 | 2685 | 2650 | 2615 | 2580 | 2545 | 2510 | 2475 | 2440 | 2405 |

Chephren's Pyramid in the foreground
with the Pyramid of Khufu behind it

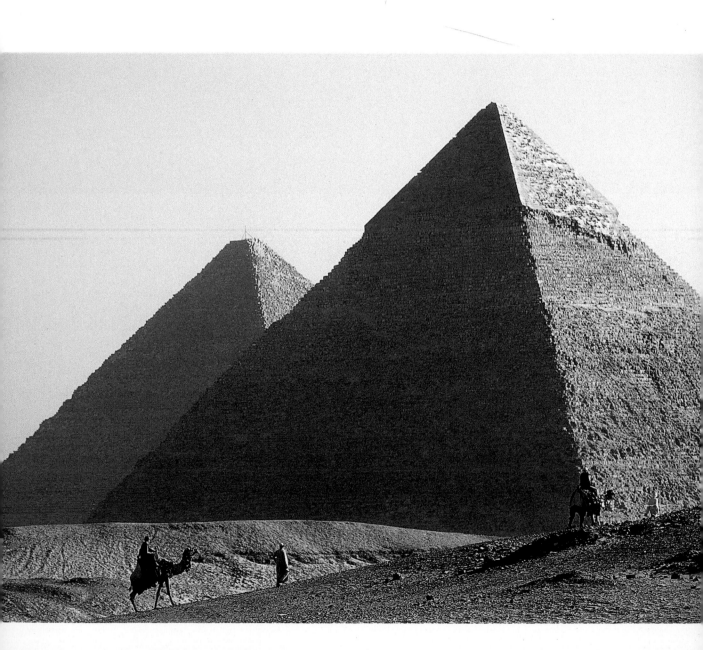

2200–1800 BC XIA DYNASTY
(FIRST DOCUMENTED CHINESE DYNASTY)

ca. 2300 BC Bronze Age begins
in Europe

3000 BC–1000 BC BRONZE AGE

2370   2335   2300   2265   2230   2195   2160   2125   2090   2055   2020   1985   1950   1915   1880   1845   1810 BC

THE GREAT PYRAMID OF GIZA

Pharaoh Khufu's tomb on the west bank of the River Nile was quite simply the largest construction in the ancient world. The pharaoh made no attempt to be modest – the most impressive of the Egyptian pyramids soars 146 metres (478 feet) above the ground.

In the third millennium BC, an entire necropolis spread over Giza, on the border with the Libyan Desert. Pharaoh Khufu (Cheops) built his own final resting place on a rock plateau 40 metres (130 feet) high only a few kilometres south-west of present-day Cairo. His father, Snofru, had already inaugurated the period of the major royal buildings: so far, more than 80 pyramids have been discovered in the Nile Valley. The Great Pyramid can be seen from a great distance, rising above the flat, desert landscape. Khufu's burial complex as a whole covers an area of over one square kilometre (about 240 acres) and is surrounded by hundreds of additional graves of his queens and important officials.

Decades of Stone upon Stone
A great many craftsmen and labourers worked for almost 30 years on Khufu's pyramid, living to the west of the building site in a temporary village. Between 2554 and 2531 BC they cut, moved and set in place 2.5 million large stone blocks to form a pyramid 210 stone courses high. Only 201 of them have survived until today as the pyramids not only fell victim to the wind and rain, but were also used by the Romans as a ready supply of building material. At the time of construction, around 5,000 stonemasons worked in the quarries to provide the rock and limestone and then build the pyramid. If the thousands of transport workers and servants are included, approximately 20,000 to 25,000 people were occupied with the construction of the Great Pyramid – one percent of the total Egyptian population of the period.

Superb Feat of Engineering
The Egyptians had acquired an extremely sophisticated building technology and advanced mathematical knowledge. The country's architects had no difficulty in calculating volumes, areas and angles with great precision, even though they used simple tools. Starting from the square base, the smooth surfaces of the pyramid's sides converge to form four triangles that meet at its peak. In spite of the sides having a base length of 230 metres (755 feet), the divergences in the construction of the pyramid are limited to a few centimetres.

Gigantic stone blocks were transported to the very centre of the construction to form the grave chamber that was to house the sarcophagus containing the embalmed body of the pharaoh. A low, sloping passageway leads downwards from the northern entrance to a large hall, where three enormous stone blocks protected the grave chamber from intruders. It was necessary to take great pains when constructing this chamber, which measures 10 x 20 Egyptian ells – or 5.2 x 10.45 metres (17 x 34 feet) – as the Egyptians believed that the pharaoh lived on eternally in his pyramid. It was also hoped that he would take care of his people from the afterlife. For this reason, he had to be well provided for: fresh air came through slender shafts, exquisite burial goods were stacked around his sarcophagus, and sacrifices were offered up to him in the Temple of the Dead at the foot of the pyramid. His happiness ensured the happiness of Egypt.

THE GREAT PYRAMID OF GIZA, EGYPT
2554–2531 BC

FACT FILE
Location South-west of Cairo
Height Almost 147 m/482 ft (today 138.8 m/455 ft)
Length of side 230 m/755 ft (today 225 m/738 ft)
Area of base Approx. 53,000 sq m/ 570,486 sq ft
Area of surface 85,500 sq m/ 920,310 sq ft
Materials Limestone, basalt and granite
Number of stone blocks Approx. 2.5 million
Estimated total weight Approx. 6.35 million tons

The Great Gallery inside Khufu's Pyramid

following double page:
The Sphinx, with the Great Pyramid of Giza in the background

2040 BC–1640 BC MIDDLE KINGDOM
IN EGYPT (11TH–12TH DYNASTIES)

1700 BC–1100 BC SHANG DYNASTY IN CHINA

1800 BC Cultivation of sunflowers and pumpkins
in eastern North America

ca. 2000 BC Stonehenge Culture in England

1760 BC City-state of Babylon
achieves local dominance

BRONZE AGE 3000 BC–1000 BC

2260 BC 2225 2190 2155 2120 2085 2050 2015 1980 1945 1910 1875 1840 1805 1770 1735 1700 1665

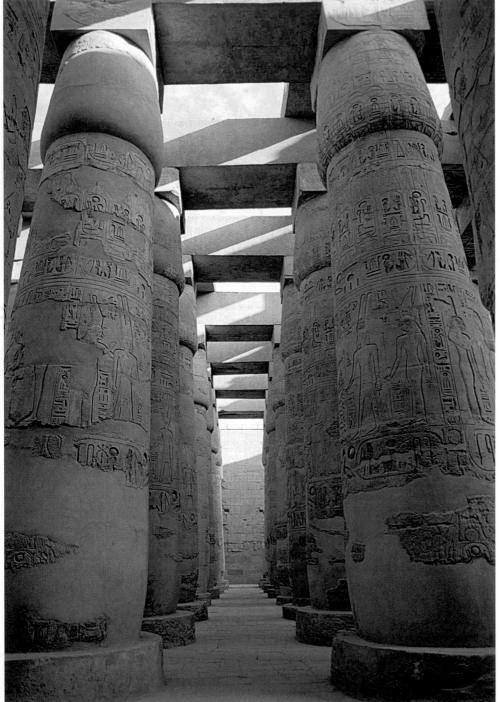

View into the roofed hall of columns

1600 BC Phoenicians use the first lettered writing

1550 BC First fortified settlements in Central
and Eastern Europe

1417 BC Peak of the prosperity and power of Egypt
under Amenophis III

1230 BC Moses leads the Israelites
out of Egypt

3000 BC–1000 BC BRONZE AGE

1630　1595　1560　1525　1490　1455　1420　1385　1350　1315　1280　1245　1210　1175　1140　1105　1070 BC

KARNAK TEMPLE

The Egyptian kingdom reached the height of its power during the second millennium BC. The country on the Nile had become the major power in the region. The New Kingdom demonstrated this power and wealth through the building of gigantic temple complexes, the finest of which are Luxor, Abu Simbel and the temple at Karnak.

In the years between 1551 and 715 BC, the Nile valley took on a new appearance. Walled temple complexes of enormous size were erected in honour of the gods and the pharaohs. In Karnak, north-east of Luxor on the right bank of the Nile, tribute was paid to Amun, the sun god, one of the most revered Egyptian deities. Numerous rulers were to be involved before the temple complex, which was begun around 1550 BC, reached its final colossal size.

The temple itself rises from a rectangular base and is surrounded by massive walls. The entrance front is decorated with monumental columns and gate towers called pylons. These serve as the entrance to the temple, and are followed by a courtyard with colonnades on both sides. A spacious, covered, columned hall was connected to a second pylon. The diameter of the supports, lined up close together in rows of three, is enormous. The column shafts and capitals are decorated with figures and vegetal ornaments. Sunlight flows into the interior through openings at the side. Additional anterooms and pylons lead into the sanctuary: the great temple of Amun with its effigy of the god.

The Temple of Temples
During the New Kingdom there was a passion for building. This becomes obvious at Karnak, where entire generations of rulers made additions. Numerous forecourts, pylons and temples, huge sculptures and obelisks, were erected. The construction received its first major enlargement during the reign of Thutmosis I, whose daughter then donated the obelisks for her father's additions. Thutmosis III added an additional magnificent columned hall in the south-west of the complex, where he was worshiped more than the god. Ramses II also could not resist making a contribution of this kind, and added a similar hall and monumental sculptures. The list goes on and on. The basic temple type of the New Kingdom was fully realized in the Amun Temple in Karnak, and in gargantuan dimensions. Processions

entered through the monumental gates and proceeded along the long axis of the temple: many of the rituals of such processions are immortalized in stone on the columns in the halls of the temple.

Notwithstanding the building passion of the Pharaohs, which was often self-serving, Karnak had one ultimate goal: for the sake of the kingdom, it was necessary to keep the gods satisfied.

KARNAK TEMPLE, EGYPT

CHARACTERISTICS
Location 3 kilometres north of Luxor
Size of the entire enclosure
　250,000 sq m/2,690,978 sq ft
Size of the Amun District
　530 x 510 x 510 x 700 m/
　1738.10 x 1673.3 x 1673.3 x 2296.7 ft
Maximum width of the pylon
　110 m/360.10 ft
Maximum height of the pylon
　40 m/131.3 ft

Section of the temple complex with
the obelisk of Queen Hatshepsut

FROM ca. 800 BC Rise of the
Greek city states

750 BC First record of the Greek alphabet

ANTIQUITY 1000 BC–AD 500

1000 BC   980   960   940   920   900   880   860   840   820   800   780   760   740   720   700   680   660

left:
The Acropolis, oil painting by
Leo von Klenze, 1846

right:
Floor plan of the Parthenon

below:
The most famous, still existing, building
of ancient Greece: the Parthenon

500 BC–432 BC PHIDIAS

490 BC–429 BC PERICLES

427 BC–347 BC PLATO

604–562 BC Nebuchadnezzar builds
the Tower of Babylon

521 BC Under Darius I, Persepolis
becomes the new capital of the
Persian Empire

ca. 450 BC Birth of the Buddha in India

334 BC Alexander the
Great ends Persian
dominance

510 BC Romans expel the Etruscan king and found the Republic
508 BC Establishment of Greek democracy

640   620   600   580   560   540   520   500   480   460   440   420   400   380   360   340   320   300 B

THE PARTHENON

When visiting Athens in 1911, the architect Le Corbusier stated that "the Parthenon, this terrible machine, turns everything within a radius of three miles to dust." This impressive marble temple on the Acropolis above Athens took no notice – it's still regarded as the epitome of Greek architecture and ancient culture, and one of the key works of Western architecture.

In the 5th century BC, Athens – and with it the surrounding region of Attica – developed into one of the largest and most powerful city-states in ancient Greece. Athens often found itself in mortal conflict with the Persians but, in the decades between 450 and 400 BC, the situation greatly improved. Athens flourished under the leadership of a charismatic leader, Pericles: the city became an important commercial centre with a wide-spread network of trading connections, and secured its influence with a large navy. And as the city-state evolved, so did its culture.

A Home for the City's Goddess

Building projects also flourished during this period. Pericles began the construction of the temple on the Acropolis (Greek for "upper-city"), which had been destroyed by the Persians. The Parthenon Temple was the major building of the prestigious project. This huge temple, built entirely of white marble, was much larger than the previous building, and yet was erected in a mere 15 years. The western front of the richly decorated building was adorned with eight Doric columns, and there were 17 columns on each of the long sides. Construction of the Parthenon, following plans by the architect Iktinos, was completed around 432 BC. It resisted the ravages of time until the late 17th century, when a shot from a Venetian cannon hit the Turkish gunpowder store in the Parthenon and destroyed a major section of the building.

The Parthenon was dedicated to the patron goddess of the city, Athena, but was not reserved solely for her. It was even more important as a place for storing the state's treasures. Through this impressive city memorial, temple and treasure house, Athens proclaimed its wealth and power. The sculptural decoration was correspondingly lavish: Pericles commissioned the sculptor Phidias, who was already famous, to carve the temple's decoration. This consisted of the sculptures on the triangular pediments at the ends of the temple, and a 160-metre (525-foot) relief frieze featuring depictions of battles, which ran around the building.

Criticism and Exile

Despite the success of the project, both Pericles and Phidias received severe criticism. Pericles was accused by his Athenian contemporaries of misusing their money for city beautification – the constructions costs amounted to five tons of silver! He was able to save himself by drawing attention to the positive results of the undertaking: above all, he had created many jobs and encouraged a revival in the arts and crafts. Phidias, however, did not get off as easily. He was accused by his co-workers of having embezzled large sums of money when he created the 12-metre (40-foot) high bronze statue of Athena, and he was finally forced to go into exile.

THE PARTHENON, ATHENS, GREECE
447–432 BC

CHRONOLOGY
447–432 BC Parthenon built
5TH C AD Consecrated as a church
15TH C Ottoman Turks take Athens
and the Parthenon becomes a
mosque
1687 Venetian troops besiege the
Acropolis; Parthenon almost
completely destroyed
EARLY 19TH C Lord Elgin sells sections
of the sculptural programme to
the British Museum in London
1896 Reconstruction begins
1897 A true-to-scale copy of the
Parthenon is erected in Nashville,
Tennessee

The Greek Temple

The ancient Greek temple typically had a rectangular plan. Its core was an elongated interior space, the cella, surrounded by a row of columns. The cultic idol stood in the cella: in the case of the Parthenon, this was the monumental statue of the goddess Athena. Elegant columns around this inner temple hall supported heavy entablatures comprising beams, friezes and cornices. The aim throughout the temple was the creation of a harmonic relationship between vertical and horizontal lines. A temple was often decorated with sculptures and relief friezes, and this decoration, as well as the temple itself, was often painted.

264–146 BC Punic Wars I–III end in the
destruction of Carthage by the Romans

123–88 BC King Mithridates II re-establishes
the Kingdom of Parthia

ANTIQUITY 1000 BC–AD 500

| | | | | | | | | | | | | | | | | |
|280 BC|265|250|235|220|205|190|175|160|145|130|115|100|85|70|55|40|25|

Site of gladiator battles:
the Coliseum in Rome

AD 9–79 EMPEROR VESPASIAN

AD 100–175 PTOLEMY, ASTRONOMER AND GEOGRAPHER

AD 79 Herculaneum and Pompeii destroyed
by the eruption of Vesuvius

AD 130 Construction of the dome
of the Pantheon in Rome

AD 235 Beginning
of the Barracks
Emperor Era

AD 45 Apostle Paul begins missionary travel
that leads him as far as Rome

AD 117 Roman Empire reaches its greatest
extent under Emperor Trajan

ca. AD 150 Beginning of the first
Germanic mass migrations

10 BC 20 AD 35 50 65 80 95 110 125 140 155 170 185 200 215 230 245

THE COLOSSEUM

"Pecunia non olet — money doesn't smell" is a saying attributed to the builder of the Colosseum, Emperor Vespasian. And actually the "latrine tax" he introduced was not a bad source of income. In any case, the Emperor didn't have to worry about money when undertaking this mammoth building project, as can be seen from the time it took to complete it — work began in AD 72, and the huge stadium was ready a mere eight years later.

Four floors rise almost 50 metres (164 feet) above the elliptical ground plan, whose greatest expanse measures a stately 188 x 156 metres (617 x 512 feet). The floors are divided into galleries and sections, and a sophisticated system of passages and entrances assured that the events, which attracted thousands of spectators, went off without a hitch. When the amphitheatre was opened, the Romans were able to enjoy a hundred days of games, all of which were free, a gift of the emperor. Fights between gladiators and animal were very popular, and the arena could even be flooded for the enactment of naval battles.

From Stadium to Stone Quarry

The last games probably took place in AD 523, and for centuries nothing much was heard of the arena to the west of the Forum Romanum. However, the mania of the Renaissance popes for grand building projects once again drew attention to Rome's ancient ruins. In fact, many of the Church Fathers had used them to supply building materials for their churches and palaces. The Colosseum was a rich source, providing not only travertine stone, but also, in particular, concrete and bricks, as well as marble, which had been used to face the lower rows of seats. Even the lead clamps that had been used to secure one stone block to the next were much sought-after by later builders. And the Colosseum was ravaged not only by the builders of the early period of modern history: it was also severely damaged by fires and earthquakes. Yet in spite of all this, around two-fifths of the building has survived.

Column Orders

From the outside, the galleries of the Colosseum are accentuated by vertical axes – arches and columns that could be straight out of the chapter on "column orders" in a Roman's "architect's handbook." In Classical architecture there are several column types, categorised according to the style of their base, shaft and (above all) capital. Plain Doric columns are found on the lower floors of the Colosseum. Ionic columns, which have more elaborate capitals, grace the second floor. The columns used for the third floor supposedly originated in the wealthy commercial centre of Corinth: the richly decorated Corinthian capital is similar to the Ionian, though with the addition of leaves and other plant motifs. Emperor Vespasian didn't survive to see the completion of the fourth floor – his son and successor, Domitian, added this after his father's death. This was not merely for aesthetic reasons: awnings to protect the crowd from the fierce sun could be attached above the small window openings. Some of the 50,000 to 70,000 spectators obviously preferred a seat in the shade.

THE COLOSSEUM, ROME, ITALY
72–80 BC

FACT FILE
Materials Brick, travertine and concrete
Total height 48.5 m/159 ft
Area Approx. 19,000 sq m/204,510 sq ft
Greatest expanse 188 x 156 m/
617 x 512 ft
Capacity Approx. 50,000–70,000
spectators
Use until 5th C AD Amphitheatre

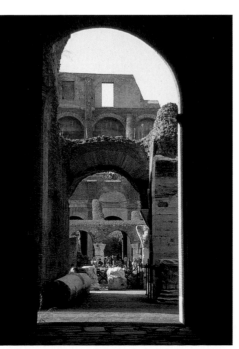

A public corridor in the Coliseum

221 BC Shi Huángdì becomes first Emperor of China;
construction of the Great Wall begins

123–88 BC King Mithridates II re-establishes
the Kingdom of Parthia

ANTIQUITY 1000 BC–AD 500

| 300 BC | 285 | 270 | 255 | 240 | 225 | 210 | 195 | 180 | 165 | 150 | 135 | 120 | 105 | 90 | 75 | 60 | 45 |

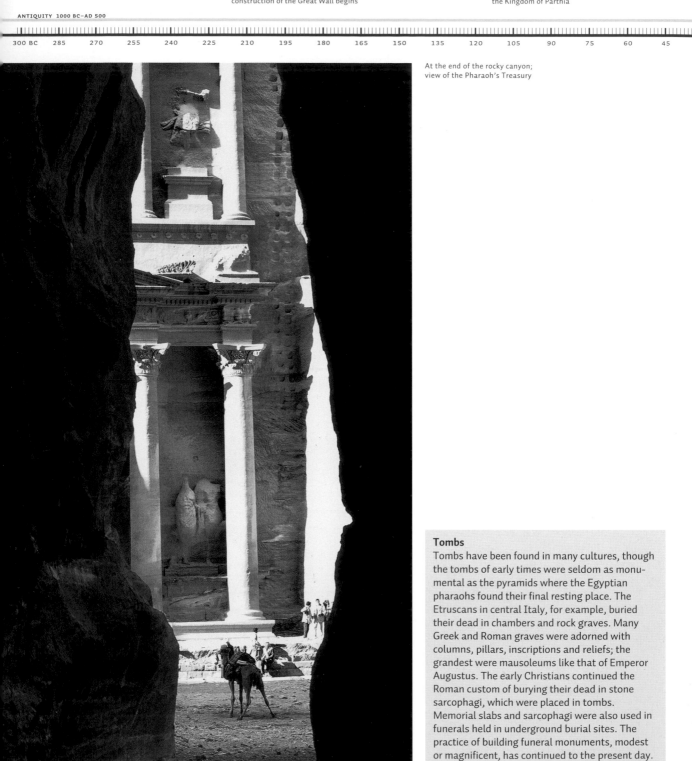

At the end of the rocky canyon;
view of the Pharaoh's Treasury

Tombs

Tombs have been found in many cultures, though the tombs of early times were seldom as monumental as the pyramids where the Egyptian pharaohs found their final resting place. The Etruscans in central Italy, for example, buried their dead in chambers and rock graves. Many Greek and Roman graves were adorned with columns, pillars, inscriptions and reliefs; the grandest were mausoleums like that of Emperor Augustus. The early Christians continued the Roman custom of burying their dead in stone sarcophagi, which were placed in tombs. Memorial slabs and sarcophagi were also used in funerals held in underground burial sites. The practice of building funeral monuments, modest or magnificent, has continued to the present day.

AD 9–79 EMPEROR
VESPASIAN

AD 100–175 PTOLEMY, ASTRONOMER AND GEOGRAPHER

AD 79 Herculaneum and Pompeii destroyed
by the eruption of Vesuvius

AD 130 Construction of the dome of the
Pantheon in Rome

AD 45 Apostle Paul begins missionary travel
that leads him as far as Rome

AD 117 Roman Empire reaches its greatest
extent under Emperor Trajan

ca. AD 150 Beginning of the first
Germanic mass migrations

AD 125 Construction of the Hadrian Wall in Great Britain under Emperor Hadrian

30   15 BC   15 AD   30   45   60   75   90   105   120   135   150   165   180   195   210   225

PETRA

More than 80 percent of Jordan is covered by stone and lava deserts, the rest by sand. So it's astonishing, in the midst of the stones in the south-west of the country, to find the remains of an ancient city. Petra was the main settlement — and later royal city — of the desert people the Nabataeans.

The culture of the Nabataeans reached its peak around 2,000 years ago. Mainly traders who constantly travelled long distances, originally the Nabataeans did not live in a precisely defiled region, and only gradually settled in permanent settlements along the Incense Road, which linked Egypt with north Arabia and India. Petra was a junction of two important desert routes. A modest trading post rapidly developed into a commercial and political centre, and the growing affluence of the city was accompanied by major building projects.

A City in the Desert

At the time of the Nabataeans, the Sik – a long, narrow and rocky gorge almost 70 metres (230 feet) high – was the main route into the city area of Petra. Once visitors had passed through the Sik, they found themselves facing an entire city literally carved out of solid sandstone. At the height of its success, approximately 10,000 people lived in this rocky desert city, whose stones shimmer in a multitude of colours from pink, shades of yellow and white, to light grey. So far, archaeologist have explored only one percent of the city area of Petra, even though the scientific investigation of the trading centre began in the early 19th century. Since then, many public buildings – including a theatre for around 8,000 spectators – have been unearthed. Excavation still continues to bring new wonders to light.

Building for a Life after Death

The deep valley of Petra is strewn with monumental tombs and orderly rows of much smaller tombs. The façades of some of the grave chambers are several metres high and occasionally span two storeys. The size and sculptural decoration of the tombs vary; some of the simpler ones are framed by flat columns, others are adorned with obelisks. To create these monuments, masons had first to create a flat surface on the stone, and then carve more three-dimensional forms, such as columns and pediments, merlons

PETRA, JORDAN
Constructed 100 BC–AD 200

The city in stone was already a popular travel destination when the American film director Steven Spielberg made it known to a much wider audience. The Sik, the narrow gorge leading into the city, was the location for the final part of his Indiana Jones trilogy. In *Indiana Jones and the Last Crusade*, the star of the film, Harrison Ford, is involved in the search for the Holy Grail. The impressive façade of the Khazne Firaun – the "Pharaoh's Treasury" – served as the background for the film's showdown.

and arches. Occasionally the façades of the tombs were decorated with plaster or coloured.

The Khazne Firaun – the "Pharaoh's Treasury" – displays the most famous façade of the city. This large building, enclosed by solid rock, was probably not a treasure house, but very little is known about its actual function, or even when it was built. The two-storey façade of the red-sandstone building rises to a height of 40 metres (131 feet). The central four of the six columns on the lower floor support a large pediment, above which there stands a round, pavilion-like structure that rises up between a large broken pediment on the upper floor. Stone sarcophagi were probably placed in the chambers in the interior of this so-called treasure house, though there is still a great deal of debate over whether the Khazne Firaun was actually a storehouse, temple or tomb.

The Khazne Firaun,
the Pharaoh's Treasury

300   Beginning of the classical period of Mayan cities such as Palenque, Uxmal and Tikal

283   The Roman region Limes Germanicus is lost to the Alemanni

330   Constantinople replaces Rome as the new capital of the Roman Empire

ANTIQUITY 1000 BC–AD 500

| 200 | 210 | 220 | 230 | 240 | 250 | 260 | 270 | 280 | 290 | 300 | 310 | 320 | 330 | 340 | 350 | 360 | 370 |

The Jaguar Temple in the Mayan city of Tikal

383 Under Emperor Theodosius I, Christianity becomes the Roman state religion | **395** Division of the Roman Empire into the Western and Eastern Roman Empires

376 Peak of the Indian Gupta Empire under Chandragupta II

ca. 400 Intensive building in Teotihuacán (Central America), which has around 400,000 inhabitants | **451** Attila, the King of the Huns, is beaten back after causing severe devastation in Central Europe

380 390 400 410 420 430 440 450 460 470 480 490 500 510 520 530 540 550

TIKAL

The remains of the ancient Mayan city of Tikal lie in the midst of the rainforests of the province of El Petén in the north of Guatemala. In the 5th century BC, the Tikal civilization covered an area of almost 64 square kilometres (25 square miles).

Research into Tikal began in the 19th century, when the site was overgrown with dense vegetation. Temples and palaces were gradually uncovered and made accessible to the public, and now Tikal is regarded as one of the best researched Mayan cities, with the power to attract both tourists and scholars.

Thriving Community

The area was already settled in the 7th century BC, but Tikal experienced its high point in the 5th century AD. More than 3,000 individual buildings, including palace complexes, squares and street, steles and water reservoirs, as well as simple living quarters, have been identified in the central area of the city, which was protected by substantial defence fortifications. At the peak of the city's development, around 75,000 persons lived in an area of approximately 15 square kilometres (six square miles). At that time, magnificent buildings were erected, together with hundreds of stone steles that record the history of the city and the deeds of its most prominent citizens. In addition, the highest temple pyramid in Mesoamerica – Temple IV, which is almost 56 metres (184 feet) high – is located in the west of Tikal.

The political heart, however, was in its centre, on the Great Plaza, which was lined with altars and temples. The ruler Hasaw Kan K'awil rests under a nine-stepped pyramid, Temple I, the Temple of the Great Jaguar, on the east side of the square. Temple II, the Mood Temple, erected on a three-tiered base, stands opposite. Both were plastered white originally, while their distinctive roof "combs" were decorated in bright colours. The largest ensemble of buildings in Tikal can be found to the north of this main square. This is the North Acropolis, which has a building history covering around 1,000 years.

Temples and tombs were erected on various levels and could be reached by steep flights of stone steps. The rulers spread themselves out over the southeast of the Great Plaza; their labyrinthine palace complex stretched over several inner courtyards and the numerous rooms of the palace were connected to each other by underground corridors. And of course Tikal, like other Mesoamerican sites, did not lack a field for ritual ballgames.

The End of a Civilization

Researchers have been successful in decoding the Maya's hieroglyphic script, and now more and more is known of the achievements of this advanced civilization, which had an extremely well-developed calendar, and whose kings included Smoke Frog, Great Jaguar Paw and Prince Chocolate. This research also made the reasons for Tikal's decline and fall much clearer. In AD 509, King Chak Tok Ich'aak II was taken prisoner and died without leaving a successor. In 562, Tikal's arch-enemy, Calakmul, conquered the city. It appears that most of the population then emigrated. By the 9th century AD, the city was completely deserted.

TIKAL, GUATEMALA
2nd–9th C AD

CHRONOLOGY
ca. 600 BC Settlements in the Tikal area
AD 378 Tikal becomes an important centre in the El Petén region
682–723 Reign of King Ah Cacao (Chocolate Prince)
ca. 800 Tikal has a population of between 80,000 and 100,000
879 Last record of the city being inhabited
1881/82 Systematic study of Tikal begins under the direction of Hiram Bingham
1950–61 Extensive excavations undertaken
SINCE 1955 National park
1979 UNESCO World Heritage Site

Temple and graves on the northern Acropolis

CLOVIS THE GREAT, KING OF THE FRANKS

JUSTINIAN, EASTERN-ROMAN EMPEROR

452 Foundation of Venice by population
from the mainland fleeing the Huns

476 Fall of the Western Roman Empire

500 First construction of the Vatican
Palace under Pope Symmachus

455 Vandals plunder Rome

ANTIQUITY 1000 BC–AD 500

1000 BC–AD 500 ANTIQUITY PRE-ROMANESQUE 500–1000

| 425 | 430 | 435 | 440 | 445 | 450 | 455 | 460 | 465 | 470 | 475 | 480 | 485 | 490 | 495 | 500 | 505 | 510 |

It is regarded as the most important
Byzantine construction: the Hagia Sophia

532	Reconstruction of Constantinople under Emperor Justinian
540	Eastern Roman Empire dominates the Mediterranean region
585	West Goths subjugate Spain

515 520 525 530 535 540 545 550 555 560 565 570 575 580 585 590 595 600

HAGIA SOPHIA

At the time of its construction, Hagia Sophia, the Church of the Holy Wisdom, was regarded as the eighth wonder of the world. For centuries, Hagia Sophia, in the heart of the cultural and commercial centre of Constantinople (today Istanbul), was by far the largest church in the Christian world.

Generations of scholars have pondered over how it was possible for 6th-century builders to construct a free-floating dome almost 56 metres (183 feet) high and 31 metres (102 feet) wide. None of the plans for the impressive domed roof, which rests on only four massive pillars, has come down to us. However, its architects are known: Anthemios of Tralles and the mathematician Isidoros of Milet were the men commissioned by Emperor Justinian I to build a new cathedral in the capital of the Eastern Roman Empire. Hagia Sophia, constructed in the mere five years between 532 and 537, unified the needs of religion (it was primarily a bishop's church) with those of the court and the state. Justinian invested the staggering amount of 145 tons of gold in the construction of the building, and – if one can believe the historian Procopios – was even actively involved in the planning and building, personally visiting the site every day to reassure himself that progress was being made.

Collapse

However, one year after the church's consecration, the dome collapsed – it had not survived for very long in an area where earthquakes are frequent. The downward thrust of the first dome caused the pillars and supporting arches to bend and they were forced outwards. The nephew of Isidoros of Milet immediately began the reconstruction: he increased the height of the buttresses, moved some of the columns, and rebuilt the walls. And, after all these changes had been implemented, the building was topped with an even higher dome, and consecrated at Christmas 562. And – if we overlook a few major and minor repairs – it has stood firm to this day.

From Church to Mosque

The design combines two basic forms of church: a "directional" basilica and a centrally planed building. The central space is dominated by the main dome, with smaller domes on the west and east. The domes, side aisles and galleries cover an area of 10,000 square metres (107,640 square feet) and were originally decorated with mosaics on a gold ground, and with sheets of white marble. Some remnants of these can still be seen. Little of the decoration of the Christian church has been preserved, however, for after the conquest of Constantinople by Sultan Mehmet II, Hagia Sophia became the main mosque of the Ottoman Empire. Christian symbols were replaced by Moslem ones, the icons were removed, and the mosaics inside the church were hidden or plastered over because of the Islamic ban on figurative images. Four minarets were constructed, and these still dominate the external appearance of this unique building, which now serves as a museum.

HAGIA SOPHIA, ISTANBUL, TURKEY
AD 532–537

FACT FILE
Builder Emperor Justinian I
Architects Anthemios of Tralles and Isidoros of Milet
Area Approx. 70 x 75 m/230 x 246 ft
Wall-surface area More than 10,000 sq m/107,640 sq ft
Height of dome Almost 56 m/184 ft
Costs Approx. 145 tons of gold
Use Originally a church, then a mosque and, since 1934, a museum

Dome
Even today, scholars are still amazed at the daring construction of the dome of Hagia Sophia. Four different possibilities exist for closing a space with this form of vaulting. In the case of the Hagia Sophia, the builders decided on a pendentive dome, in which a round dome sits on a square base. The curving triangles that are formed by the transition from the square base to the circular dome are called pendents, or hanging spandrels. A circular opening at the top of the dome allows light to fall into the vast space below.

The cupola and four minarets,
taken against the light

right page:
The interior of the Hagia Sophia: built
as a Christian church, transformed into
a mosque and used today as a museum

452 Foundation of Venice by population
         from the mainland fleeing the Huns

476 End of the Western-Roman Empire

ANTIQUITY 1000 BC–AD 500   1000 BC–AD 500 ANTIQUITY   PRE-ROMANESQUE 500–1000

435   440   445   450   455   460   465   470   475   480   485   490   495   500   505   510   515   520

External view of the Basilica of
San Vitale

below:
View into the octagonal cupola of
San Vitale with its magnificent mosaic
decorations

529 Foundation of European monastic life by
St Benedict of Nursia

540 Eastern-Roman Empire dominates the Mediterranean region

585 West Goths
subjugate Spain

586 Establishment of the Lombard realm
in northern and central Italy

ca. 600 Mass migration decreases

525   530   535   540   545   550   555   560   565   570   575   580   585   590   595   600   605   610

SAN VITALE

Constantinople (today Istanbul in Turkey) had developed into an important cultural centre following the division of the Roman Empire. In the 6th century AD, Emperor Justinian pushed forward with his plans to expand the East Roman Empire, and the Byzantines conquered the small northern Italian city of Ravenna in 526. They stayed 200 years, and clearly left their mark.

In the very same year, the new ruler laid the foundation stone for the Church of San Vitale. The building has an octagonal central section in front of which there's a vestibule. The dome, also octagonal, and with a diameter of 16 metres (52 feet), forms a vault over the central room. The central area is surrounded by an ambulatory, with light flowing in through round-arched windows. The ambulatory rises over two storeys; galleries vaulted over by half-domes are located on the upper storey, and both storeys open to the interior through high Norman arches. The external appearance of the church, which was completed in 547, is dominated by simple brickwork, and the dome is covered by a modest roof in the form of a low, many-sided pyramid. The interior of San Vitale, however, is a different story.

Glorious Mosaics
The mosaic decoration of the central building begins immediately above the high marble base. The adornment on the walls of San Vitale is one of the few surviving examples of Byzantine mosaic art dating from late antiquity. The greater portion of the decoration of the churches fell victim to the iconoclasts of the 8th and 9th centuries, who destroyed religious images considered to be impious.

However, the pictorial programme in San Vitale is still easy to interpret. Scenes from the New and Old Testaments face each other. Above the window area of the back wall, we see Christ enthroned between saints and archangels. In the semi-circular end of the altar room, the apse, the mosaics are particularly impressive. These images, which also adorn the vaulted ceiling, appear to be covered with a golden shimmer.

The walls are peopled with angels and saints, and the alcoves and walls are decorated with architectural depictions and vegetal and geometric ornamentation. Countless tesserae – small cubes of coloured glass or stone used in mosaic – contribute to the glorious impression created by the interior, which is further enhanced by the light falling through the high windows.

Emperor Charlemagne seems to have been less impressed by the magnificent decoration than by the octagonal form, and was greatly inspired by this Italian church when constructing his chapel in Aachen around AD 800 (see pages 36–39).

SAN VITALE, RAVENNA, ITALY
AD 526–547

CHARACTERISTICS
Diameter of the dome 16 m/53 ft
Consecration April 19, 548
Addition to the UNESCO World Heritage List 1996

The apse with the enthroned Christ

KHOSRAU II, KING OF
THE SASSANID EMPIRE

HERACLIUS I,
EASTERN ROMAN EMPEROR

OMAR IBN AL-KHATTAB,
ARABIAN CALIPH

600 Peak of Mayan culture in
South America

618 Tang dynasty rules the new Chinese Empire

570 Birth of the Prophet
Mohammed

586 Establishment of the Lombard realm
in northern and central Italy

606 Major Indian empire
under Harshavardhana
of Kannauj

622 Introduction of Moslem calendar

PRE-ROMANESQUE 500–1000

555   560   565   570   575   580   585   590   595   600   605   610   615   620   625   630   635   640

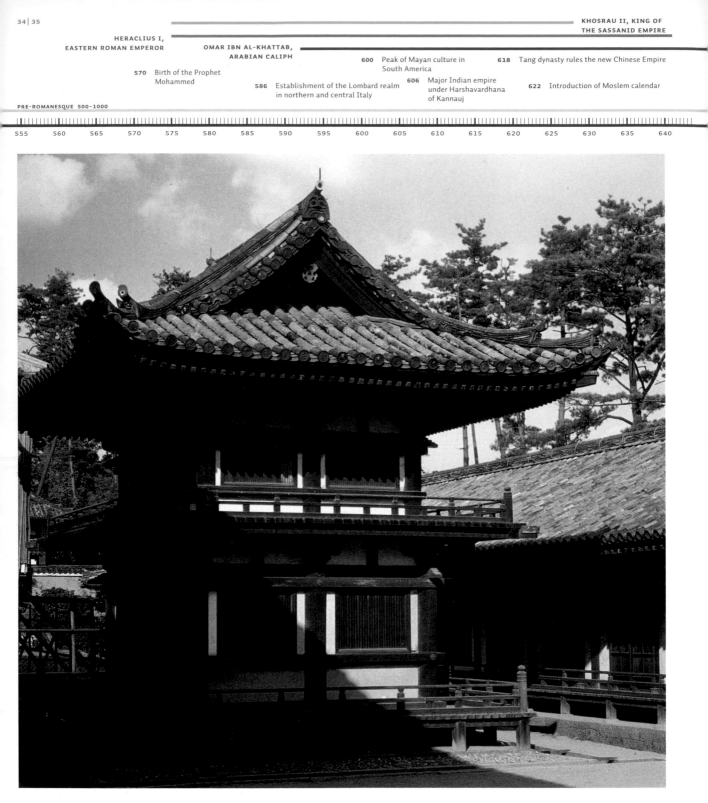

Architecture from the early years of
Buddhism: The Horyuji Temple complex

right page:
The Kondu, the main hall and one of the
oldest preserved wooden constructions

661 Umayyad Dynasty establishes a major Arab
empire (Umayyad Caliphate)

692 Construction of the Islamic Dome
of the Rock in Jerusalem

710 Nara becomes Japanese capital

645   650   655   660   665   670   675   680   685   690   695   700   705   710   715   720   725   730

HORYUJI TEMPLE

Created at the beginning of the 7th century AD, the Horyuji is the oldest Buddhist temple complex in Japan.
It is also the only completely preserved sacred building from the early period of Buddhist architecture.

Buddhism made its way to Japan from China and Korea in the middle of the 6th century AD. The Japanese court regarded the new religion as an opportunity for uniting the country and for strengthening their own power; major construction works soon followed. The impressive temple complexes that resulted had a new and distinctive architectural form: they were built around a hall placed on a platform with its supports and the roof resting on wooden columns.

A Buddhist Prince

The Horyuji Temple, located 10 kilometres (6 miles) south-west of Nara in the south of the main island of Japan, is a product of this early stage of Buddhist architecture. Prince Shotoku, a declared admirer of Buddhism, had work on the temple started in the year 607. Under his rule, many Korean labourers went to Japan to construct and decorate the numerous temples. Shotoku paid particular attention to two complexes: the Shitennoji Temple, in what is today Osaka, and his first building project, Horyuji.

The temple area at Horyuji is surrounded by a wall. In the west, a two-tiered gate leads into the interior. The most important of the 31 buildings in the complex are located in the western section of the temple. The eastern temple sector was erected in the 8th century and consists of 14 buildings. The heart of this smaller complex is the octagonal Yumedono, the Hall of Dreams, where the body of the princely founder of the temple rests.

A Masterpiece in Wood

The main building in the western section, the Kodo, or Golden Hall, which consists of two storeys built over a rectangular plan, is the oldest wooden building in the world. The posts that support the massive roof are painted a reddish-brown, while the walls in between are plastered white. The heart of the building is a richly decorated room – called the *moya* – containing an altar and shrines. The

verandas, the *hisashi*, which lead around this central room, are covered by a protruding roof.

After a fire had destroyed large sections of the building in 670, it was reconstructed in the original style using cypress wood. At that time, the pagoda was moved and, since then, has been located to the left of the Golden Hall, which disturbs the symmetry of the original plan. The five-tiered pagoda is also ancient; in fact it's the oldest in Japan. A reading room in the north closes the inner area of the temple. Over the centuries, additional buildings, including two modern treasuries, have found their way into the Horyuji ensemble.

HORYUJI TEMPLE, NARA, JAPAN
Start of construction, 7th C AD

The history of the Horyuji Temple dates back to a vow of Emperor Yōmei. Out of thanks for his recovery from illness, Yōmei had promised to erect a temple and statue of Buddha. He died, however, before he could put his plan into action. The crown prince Shōtoku and Empress Suiko fulfilled Yōmei's last wish and began to build the temple. In 1993, the Temple site became the first Japanese monument to be added to the UNESCO World Heritage List.

711 Arabs conquer the West Gothic
kingdom in Spain

732 Charles Martel beats back the Arab
army near Poitiers

751–843 Carolingian Empire

PRE-ROMANESQUE 500–1000

| 675 | 680 | 685 | 690 | 695 | 700 | 705 | 710 | 715 | 720 | 725 | 730 | 735 | 740 | 745 | 750 | 755 | 760 |

It forms the centre of the Aachen Minster:
Charlemagne's Palatine Chapel

800 Charlemagne crowned emperor

FROM 793 Viking raids along European coasts
and river courses

ca. 770 Chang-àn, capital of the Chinese Tang
empire with about one million inhabitants

802 Foundation of the Angkor dynasty
by Emperor Jayavarman

843 Division of the
Carolingian Empire

765   770   775   780   785   790   795   800   805   810   815   820   825   830   835   840   845   850

PALATINE CHAPEL IN AACHEN

One of the major building complexes of the Middle Ages, the palace complex at Aachen in Germany, provided all that an emperor needed: fortified living accommodation, storerooms, fine reception areas and a chapel. The emperor didn't have permanent residence, so he had to move continuously throughout his large kingdom. His various palaces served not only practical needs: they were a direct and very visible expression of his power.

Most of the buildings at Aachen are known only from excavations. In fact, only one building has survived intact – but this, fortunately, is its remarkable chapel. Aachen was located in the east of Emperor Charlemagne's realm, and his decision to erect his most important palace at this seemingly insignificant location may be connected with the warm thermal springs there, which had already been appreciated by the Romans.

The Chapel and Imperial Power
Construction of the imperial palace began just after 790. Extensive outbuildings, which guaranteed that provisions were available for the travelling court, were part of the living complexes, as was a fine reception room.

The chapel is entered by an impressive portal on its western side. The main domed room is a two-storey octagon with a diameter of almost 20 metres (65 feet). A large choir is attached on the east side. Arches open the octagon to the vaulted 16-sided ambulatory. Galleries are located on the upper floor behind arches supported by tall, slender columns. Some of the columns and capitals in the upper church are spolia, in other words material taken from ancient ruins. Charlemagne was not satisfied with just any old pieces; he had selected treasures delivered to him from Ravenna in Italy (see pages 32–33). This was the Emperor's way of creating a direct link with the magnificent buildings of the last capital city of the West Roman Empire. He had obtained the Pope's personal permission to carry off columns from the palace in Ravenna to Aachen. Set very visibly in the Aachen chapel, these *spolia* stress the importance of the church in which Charlemagne's throne stood.

From Chapel to Cathedral
Odo von Metz has been identified as the architect of the chapel at Aachen, but that is all that is known about him. The building was consecrated in 805 by an illustrious person – Pope Leo III himself travelled all the way from Rome to the remote town for this very purpose. Nine years later, Emperor Charlemagne was buried there.

For more than 200 years, Charlemagne's chapel was the tallest building north of the Alps. A lot has happened to it since then, and today the octagon forms the centre of Aachen Cathedral. A gothic choir and chapels were added, and the interior decoration changed. At the end of the 18th century, Napoleon had the ancient spolia columns removed to Paris. However, with the exception of four that are still in the Louvre, they have since been returned to Aachen.

PALATINE CHAPEL, AACHEN, GERMANY
ca. 790–800

Under Charles the Great (748-848), Art, Literature and Architecture experienced a boom, and the period in which he reigned is called the Carolinian Renaissance. Under his government, the cloisters St Gallen, Reichenau and Tergensee became considerably more important. In 1978, the Aachen Cathedral and the Palatine Chapel became the first German monuments to be added to the UNESCO World Heritage List.

Floor plan of the Palantine Chapel and the adjoining constructions

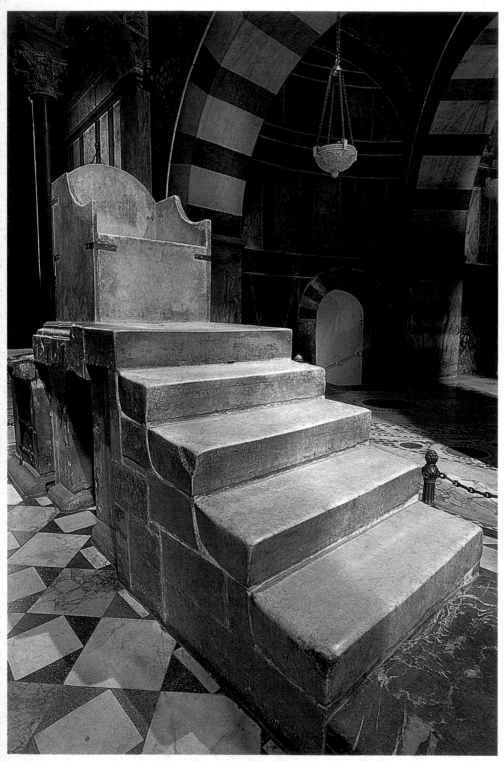

The *cathedra regalis*: The Kings were
crowned on this simple marble throne

right page:
The interior of the octagon with the low
ambulatory and gallery

711 Arabs conquer the West Gothic kingdom in Spain

732 Charles Martel beats back the Arab army near Poitiers

ca. 770 Chang-àn, capital of the Chinese Tang Empire with about one million inhabitants

751–843 Carolingian Empire in Central Europe

PRE-ROMANESQUE 500–1000

700   705   710   715   720   725   730   735   740   745   750   755   760   765   770   775   780   785

Aerial view from the north

below:
The upper platform with the circular terraces

BASIL I, BYZANTINE EMPEROR

786 Baghdad becomes a centre of art and
learning under Caliph Harun ar-Rashid

800 Charlemagne crowned Emperor

802 Foundation of the Angkor dynasty by Emperor Jayavarman

794 Kyoto replaces Nara as Japanese capital

824 Unified Anglo-Saxon state comes
into existence

850 The Maya leave the southern lowlands of
Mexico and move to Yucatan

790 795 800 805 810 815 820 825 830 835 840 845 850 855 860 865 870 875

BOROBUDUR

Monastery, burial place or simply a symbol of power? Borobudur's real function is still a matter of dispute. However, there is general consent that this temple, in the centre of the Indonesian island of Java, represents a Buddhist meditation image (mandala) of colossal size.

The work involved was enormous. Labourers fitted together two million stone blocks to form a vast pyramid without leaving the slightest space between them. The seven-tiered temple rises above a square base, the side of which measure 113 metres (370 feet). The lower zone is formed by four square galleries, the upper zone by three round terraces, all constructed of unplastered stone. The stairs and step-like gates connect the different levels. The three concentric circles support a total of 72 stupas, each of them with a seated figure of the Buddha, with the large central stupa crowning the highest tier.

Sleeping for a Thousand Years

The Borobudur temple was built around AD 800, during the reign of the Shailendra kings. Their period of rule over central Java is impressively recorded by the remarkable Borobudur temple, which was reached by a pilgrimage route lined with other temples. The Candi Pawon and Candi Menut complexes, located in the immediate vicinity of the mother temple, are considerably smaller but just as richly decorated with reliefs. Despite its overwhelming size, Borobudur soon fell into oblivion, and was uncovered from beneath the tropical vegetation only at the beginning of the 19th century. Sadly, its rediscovery meant that it was soon being looted for stone and art treasures. For this reason, extravagant security measures were implemented in the 1970s. And in order to ensure its structural safety, the entire temple was dismantled, the earth beneath it stabilized, and Borobudur painstakingly rebuilt.

Journey to Enlightenment

Since then, the oversized mandala has once again greeted thousands of visitors. In the Buddhist religion, mandalas are designs, made up largely of overlapping squares and circles, representing the spiritual universe. Borobudur depicts this map of this universe precisely, its squares and circles represent different stages in the journey to Enlightenment. Numerous pilgrims still visit Borobudur each day, and if they pace around the terraces of the building in a clockwise direction they may find their way to Nirvana, the final stage of enlightenment.

Their journey is graphically illustrated in the many stories depicted on the stone reliefs – 2.5 kilometres (1.5 miles) of them in all – which decorate the inner walls of the gallery-like ambulatory. The life of the historic Buddha is depicted on the lower level, together with scenes from the everyday life in 8th- and 9th-century Java. Higher up, the chaos of human existence is left behind and pilgrims enter the realm of eternal bliss. The pictorial programme here consists of around 1,500 scenes. After this picture book in stone, it's not only Nirvana that awaits visitors – but also the throng of tourists in the archaeological park at the foot of the temple!

BOROBUDUR, JAVA, INDONESIA
ca. 800

The significance of the name Borobudur cannot be clearly defined. It most likely refers to a combination of the terms *bara* and *budur*. *Bara* could come from *Vihara*, a Javanese designation for a complex of temples or cloisters.

Buddha figure; its gesture shows the Dharmacakra Mudrā, which symbolizes the "Turning of the Wheel of Learning"

890–1081 Peak period of the Byzantine
Empire (Macedonian Dynasty)

900 Foundation of the Toltek capital city Tula
(Central America) by Topiltzin

928 Córdoba becomes a caliphate

889 Khmer King Indravarman I

936 Caliphs of Baghdad lose their power

PRE-ROMANESQUE 500–1000

| | | | | | | | | | | | | | | | | | | |
|870|875|880|885|890|895|900|905|910|915|920|925|930|935|940|945|950|955|

The Mezquita, built as a mosque is,
today, the Cathedral of Córdoba

HENRY II,
HOLY ROMAN EMPEROR

KNUT THE GREAT, KING OF ENGLAND,
NORWAY, DENMARK AND SCOTLAND

976 Beginning of construction of
St Mark's in Venice

1000 Normans land on the coast of
North America

1031 Beginning of the Reconquista (re-conquest) of
Spain from the Arabs

500–1000 PRE-ROMANESQUE   ROMANESQUE 1000–1150

960   965   970   975   980   985   990   995   1000   1005   1010   1015   1020   1025   1030   1035   1040   1045

THE MEZQUITA

Under Islamic rule, the Iberian Peninsula experienced a cultural flowering in the fields of art and architecture that lasted well into the 11th century. The Mezquita, the Grand Mosque, in Córdoba – one of the largest Islamic sacred buildings in the world – was erected in just one year.

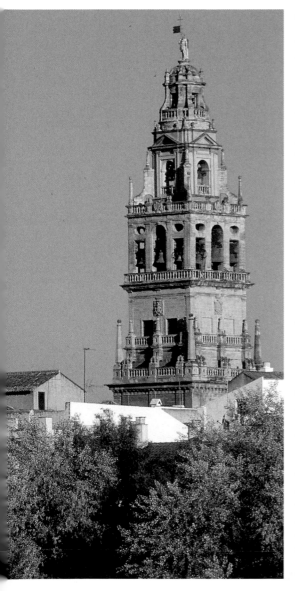

Andalusia had seen a broad range of building projects under Islamic rule. In the 10th century, there were over half a million inhabitants in Córdoba alone, which had more than 300 mosques, the same number of public baths, 50 hospitals, 80 public schools, 20 libraries and 17 universities. The Mezquita rises above the centre of the old city of Córdoba, overlooking the River Guadalquivir. It resembles a fortress: its high sandstone walls are crowned with battlements and buttresses, the whole building being set on a large rectangular base measuring 175 metres (575 feet) in length, and 128 metres (420 feet) in breadth.

In the Forest of Columns

The main entrance to the mosque, the Puerta del Pérdon, is on the northern side next to the bell tower where, originally, a minaret stood. Fountains for the ritual ablutions of the faithful were located in the Orange Courtyard, which is surrounded by arcades. Countless arcades run through the interior of the mosque. Their horseshoe-shaped arches are two-toned (made of red brick and light sandstone) and rest on simple columns. Under Abd ar-Rahman I, the Mezquita already had 11 naves with 12 vaulted bays. His successors continued with construction until the building ultimately reached a size many times greater than that of the original. In the 16th century, an enormous cathedral was built in the centre of the former mosque, which had to sacrifice four rows of arches.

Lavish Decoration

The prayer alcove, the *mihrab*, on the south wall of the Mezquita is especially magnificent. Al-Hakam II, who speeded up the extension of the mosque around 960, paid personal attention to this. He asked the Byzantine Emperor to send him a mosaic artist to instruct the local craftsmen in this technique. He came – and brought with him the 16 tons of stone material necessary for framing

MEZQUITA, CÓRDOBA, SPAIN
From AD 785

FACT FILE
Construction time Approx. 900 years
   (with interruptions)
Length 175 m/574 ft
Width 128 m/420 ft
Total area 24,000 sq m/258,334 sq ft
Number of chapels More than 50
Number of columns More than 1,000
Function Since 1236, Catholic church

The interior of the Mezquita has more than 1000 individual pillars, made out of granite, marble, onyx and jasper. The structure, along with the historic centre of Córdoba, was added to the UNESCO World Heritage List in 1984.

Detail of a mosaic in the Great Mosque

Mosques

There is no single form for the Muslim place of worship, the mosque. However, a columned hall (*haram*) is frequently a central element. A prayer alcove (*mihrab*) is inserted into the back wall (*kibla*) of the place of worship, which is always oriented towards Mecca. It is usually flanked by columns that support an arch and provide a place for the prayer leader (the *imam*) to stand when reading from the Koran or preaching. There is often a courtyard in front of the hall of columns, frequently also surrounded by pillars, with fountains for ritual washing. Another important feature of Muslim sacred buildings is the tall, tower-like minaret, from where the faithful are called to prayers.

the octagonal prayer alcove. Since then, mosaics in an unending array of colours have glittered upon the golden ground. The most important element in the *mihrab*, as in Islamic art in general, is calligraphy. The depiction of God is forbidden in Islam and so ornaments and written characters are important forms of decorative expression. Arabic calligraphy is a major ornamental motif not only in architecture, but also in ceramics, metal work and textiles.

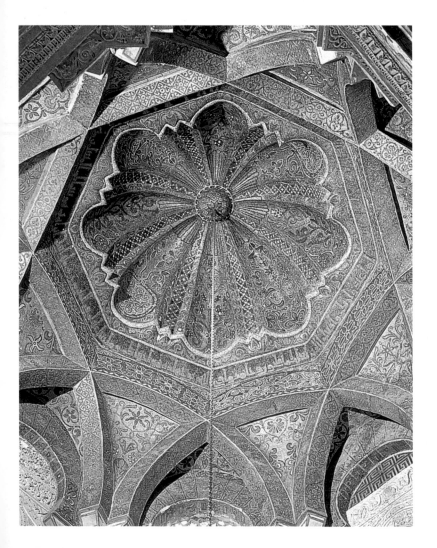

View into the vaulting above the *mihrab*

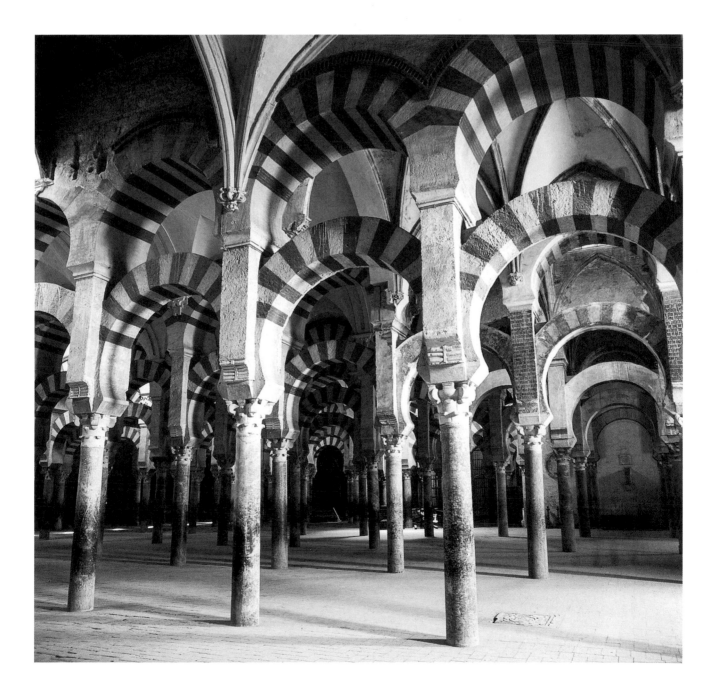

1030 Beginning of construction of the
Speyer Cathedral

1066 Battle of Hastings, Normans
conquer England

1078 Beginning of construction
of the Tower of London

ROMANESQUE 1000–1150

| 1005 | 1010 | 1015 | 1020 | 1025 | 1030 | 1035 | 1040 | 1045 | 1050 | 1055 | 1060 | 1065 | 1070 | 1075 | 1080 | 1085 | 1090 |

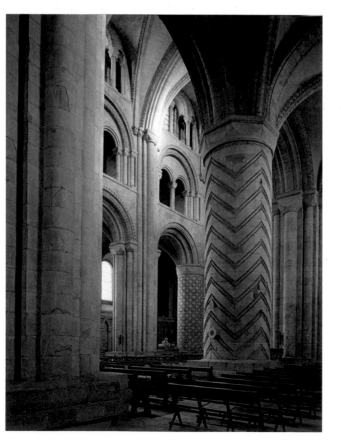

Overall view of the cathedral from the
north with the massive crossing tower

below:
Monumental columns with zigzag
patterns in the interior

1099 Jerusalem conquered by the crusaders
1100 Cliff dwellings in Mesa Verde, North America
1110 Song China most progressive and prosperous state on earth

1154 Construction of Chartres Cathedral

1000 1150 ROMANESQUE   GOTHIC 1150–1450

1095 1100 1105 1110 1115 1120 1125 1130 1135 1140 1145 1150 1155 1160 1165 1170 1175 1180

DURHAM CATHEDRAL

The Benedictine abbey in the small town of Durham in the north of England has monks from the nearby island of Lindisfarne to thank for its foundation. Fearing attacks from the Vikings, they left their island monastery in the 10th century and sought a suitable resting place for the remains of their illustrious predecessor, St Cuthbert.

After long years of searching, they were finally successful. To this very day, the relics of the bishop rest in Durham cathedral, which stands on a cliff overlooking the city centre and the River Wear. There, on the impressive site at the highest point of Durham, work on the monumental cathedral was begun in 1093. The cathedral that was built reflects both the power of the Bishops of Durham, and also the popularity of the St Cuthbert, who attracted huge numbers of pilgrims.

Saints or Sinners
This Romanesque basilica, which is 143 metres (470 feet) long, is characterized by mighty walls and massive round arches. The impressive west front is dominated by two towers, and a huge tower rises over the crossing, where the nave and transepts meet. The grave of St Cuthbert is located in the choir at the eastern end of the cathedral. The cathedral became very popular, and it was not only the numerous pilgrims who were able to count on a friendly welcome: any criminal who reached the bronze lion's-head door opener on the north-west portal could rely on being granted asylum – even murderers.

Romanesque and Gothic
The impression created by the interior is one of power and size. Monumental pillars, with a circumference of up to six metres (20 feet), support the powerful round arches of the lower section. These columns are decorated with a variety of patterns, including the zigzag forms typical of Norman design. A knowledge of the technology needed to build large-scale churches had come to England in the wake of the Norman conquest in 1066. Following the invasion, the Norman style of building (Romanesque) became widespread in England.

However, the builders of Durham Cathedral didn't simply take on a well-known architectural art form: they made their own advances, some of which anticipated the Gothic style. This is seen above all in its vaulted choir, where work began around 1100 and took 30 years to complete. The design was novel: here the weight is carried not by heavy, round arches but by vaults in which thin ribs form a framework that becomes the load-bearing structure. The spaces in between the ribs are lightly filled. The lightness and elegance of this form of structure, which is known as ribbed vaulting, forms a strong contrast to the massive Romanesque forms in the rest of the cathedral. It was here, in Durham Cathedral, that ribbed vaulting, which would be important in the development of Gothic structures, was first used successfully.

Romanesque
The characteristic art and architecture of France, Spain, Italy, Germany and England from around 1000 to 1250 was Romanesque. Introduced in the 19th century, this term was intended to describe a return to the building forms of ancient Rome. Even though there are marked regional differences in the architecture of the Romanesque, there are some important common features, notably round (Norman) arch, and thick walls with small windows. In the Romanesque era, the basilica, essentially a long nave with broad side aisles, became the preferred form for church construction. Many Romanesque churches and monasteries were richly decorated with sculptures and ornaments. The principal secular buildings during this era were castles and palaces.

DURHAM CATHEDRAL, ENGLAND
From 1093

CHRONOLOGY
BEFORE 1133 Choir, nave and transept built
ca. 1100 Choir vaulted
1170–75 Galilee Chapel in the west of the cathedral added
13TH C East transept built
1217–26 West tower front built
1242–80 Nine Altar Chapel in the east of the cathedral added
1465–90 Transept tower rebuilt after being struck by lightning
1650 Becomes a camp for Scottish prisoners of war
1986 UNESCO World Heritage Site

Information on Durham Cathedral can be found on its Internet site at http://www.durhamcathedral.co.uk/

View from the cloister towards the west towers

1030 Beginning of construction of
the Speyer Cathedral

1050 First documentation of
Nuremberg

1066 Battle of Hastings, England
conquered by the Normans

1099 Jerusalem conquered
by the crusaders

ROMANESQUE 1000–1150

1020   1025   1030   1035   1040   1045   1050   1055   1060   1065   1070   1075   1080   1085   1090   1095   1100   1105

FRIEDRICH I, BARBAROSSA,
HOLY ROMAN EMPEROR

RICHARD I, THE LION-HEART, KING OF ENGLAND

1137 Beginning of construction at St Denis
near Paris (first Gothic elements)

1000–1150 ROMANESQUE GOTHIC 1150–1450

1110 1115 1120 1125 1130 1135 1140 1145 1150 1155 1160 1165 1170 1175 1180 1185 1190 1195

THE HRADČANY

*Construction of the Hradčany, high above the River Vltava in Prague, began as early as the end of the
9th century AD. It served as an easily defended palace for the country's princes: a castle eventually surrounded
by a ring wall. It grew with each successive generation, and soon the Bishop of Prague joined the princes.
Since 1918, the castle over the Vltava has also been the official residence of the President of the Czech Republic.*

Over the centuries, many very different builders left
their traces on the Hradčany, so that late Gothic
vaults can be admired along with Baroque and
Neo-Classical features. The sturdy castle walls
shield three inner courtyards. The first, located at
the entrance to Hradčany Square, was created in the
middle of the 18th century and is the most recent.
The second, situated behind the imposing Matthias
Gate, was built during the Renaissance and the
Baroque and clearly reflects their architectural
styles.

Gothic Origins

Initially, life in the castle was confined mainly to the
third courtyard. The most magnificent building in
the Hradčany, St Vitus Cathedral, stands on its
northern side. In 1344, shortly after Pope Clement VI
had declared Prague an Episcopal See, the cornerstone for a Gothic cathedral of impressive dimensions was laid. The French architect Matthias of
Arras was responsible for planning a choir that is
47 metres (154 feet) long and almost 40 metres
(130 feet) high. After his death, the master builder
Peter Parler, who was only 23 years old at the time,
was commissioned to continue the construction.
Parler, and later his sons, not only completed the
choir and introduced a new system of vaulting,
but also immortalized themselves in the church's
interior: along with the royal family, the stone
busts of the builders look down on the visitors from
between the arcades and windows. However, not
even the Parlers were able to complete the Prague
Cathedral – this did not occur until the beginning
of the 20th century.

A Fall and its Consequences

The royal palace, which is located on the east side
of the third and oldest courtyard, acted as the seat
of the sovereign until the 16th century. It too has a
very complicated building history, for each ruler
undertook extensions and renovations. In the 15th
century, the Riders' Staircase was built for the participants of tournaments: it made it possible for the
knights to ride directly into the Vladislav Hall. The
62-metre (200-foot) long room on the second floor
of the building is made elegant by its extraordinary
vaulting.

One room in the south-east of the palace complex
is more infamous than famous. In 1618, the imperial
governors and their secretaries were thrown out of
a window of the small room into the moat. Despite
falling 15 metres (50 feet), they survived. However,
the political consequences of the revolution were
grave: this second "Defenestration of Prague" (there
had been an earlier one in 1419) led to the Bohemian
uprising against the Habsburg emperor and so,
ultimately, to the catastrophic Thirty Years' War.

**HRADČANY, PRAGUE,
CZECH REPUBLIC**
Beginning of construction 9th C AD

Peter Parler

The main cathedral architect Peter
Parler came from Schwäbisch Gmünd,
but lived primarily in Prague after the
middle of the 14th century. He spent
his period of training in the Cologne
Domhütte and, along with other
members of the Parler family, he was
responsible for the construction of
the Holy Cross Church of Münster in
Schwäbisch Gmünd until he took over
the construction of St Vitus.

left page:
The Vladislav Hall where tournaments
and festivities took place

The choir of St Vitus Cathedral

View of the Hradčany

1066 Battle of Hastings, England
conquered by the Normans

1096 Pogroms against Jewish communities in Central Europe

1081 Beginning of construction of the
Romanesque cathedral in Mainz

1122 Construction of the
Freiburg Minster

1100 Cliff dwellings in Mesa Verde, North America

ROMANESQUE 1000–1150

| 1040 | 1045 | 1050 | 1055 | 1060 | 1065 | 1070 | 1075 | 1080 | 1085 | 1090 | 1095 | 1100 | 1105 | 1110 | 1115 | 1120 | 1125 |

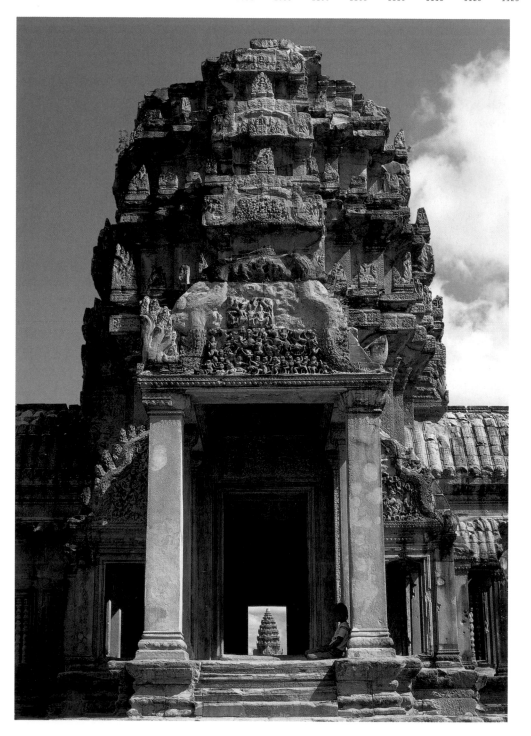

The towers of Angkor Wat are in the
form of lotus buds

RICHARD I, THE LION-HEART, KING OF ENGLAND

1137 Beginning of construction at St Denis
near Paris (first Gothic elements)

1155 Frederick I, *Barbarossa*, becomes Emperor

1200 Inca settle near Cuzco in
the Andes

1000–1150 ROMANESQUE GOTHIC 1150–1450

| 1130 | 1135 | 1140 | 1145 | 1150 | 1155 | 1160 | 1165 | 1170 | 1175 | 1180 | 1185 | 1190 | 1195 | 1200 | 1205 | 1210 | 1215 |

ANGKOR WAT

The world's largest temple complex was hidden under tropical vegetation for centuries. It was not until the 19th century that this masterpiece of the Khmer Empire, buried beneath tree roots and luxuriant foliage, once again saw the light of day. With its hundreds of small temples, pools, canals and rich sculptural decoration, Cambodia's most famous sacred building is undoubtedly one of the wonders of world architecture.

In the 9th century AD, the Khmer, the people living in what is now Cambodia, increased in importance and power in South-East Asia. Ultimately, their empire extended far beyond the borders of present-day Cambodia to incorporate parts of Vietnam and Thailand, reaching its peak between the 11th and 13th centuries. Trading boomed, waterways were cut, and a sophisticated irrigation programme made rice farming the economic basis for the population. To reflect this affluence and power, work began on an enormous temple complex, Angkor Wat (or Vat).

A Temple City is Born

It was probably during the reign of King Suraya-varman I in the first half of the 12th century AD that the Khmer began the construction of Angkor Wat, which is situated between the great lakes and Mount Kulen, to the south of the old capital, Angkor Thom. Angkor means "main city", a fact reflected in the dimensions the project assumed during the 37 years of its construction. Thousands of labourers, stonemasons, landscape designers, sculptors and architects planned and built the complex out of sandstone, surrounding the site with moats used for both transport and irrigation. Today, not one name is known from the multitude of men who built the complex, which measures 1,300 x 1,500 metres (4,260 x 4,920 feet).

The principal axis of Angkor Wat runs from west to east, with the main gate being located in the west. The central temple tower rises above a base of 365 x 250 metres (1,179 x 820 feet) and its three tiers reach a height of 65 metres (214 feet). Four additional towers surround it.

The Seat of the Gods

The walls encircling Angkor Wat, along which processions once made their way, are richly decorated with stone reliefs. These depict mythological and historical scenes from Hinduism and Buddhism, wars, victories over demons, scenes in heaven and hell. This mythology is not restricted to these external walls: the entire Angkor Wat complex is a representation of the Hindu concept of the cosmos. The world is shown as a square surrounded by mountains (walls and temples) and infinite oceans (pools). The rich symbolism of the site, both in its very structure and in its many images, has given rise to endless debate and speculation. In terms of overall function, it's clear that Angkor Wat was consecrated to the god Vishnu and the god-king Jayavarman II. It is also beyond doubt that this temple complex is a tribute to the sophisticated engineering and artistic skills of the Khmer.

ANGKOR WAT, CAMBODIA
Beginning of construction 12th C

FACT FILE
Area 1,300 x 1,500 m/4,260 x 4,920 ft
Sculptural decoration Reliefs cover more
than 1,000 sq m/10,760 sq ft
Use Temple

Maps of the location of the individual temples, as well as information on the construction and historical background, can be found at:
http://theangkorguide.com/

The silhouette of the temple mountain
of Angkor Wat; in keeping with Hindu
beliefs, it represents the blueprint of the
cosmos

1081 Beginning of construction of the
Romanesque cathedral in Mainz

1115 Robert of Molesme founds the Cistercian Order in Clairvaux

1099 Jerusalem conquered by the crusaders

1154–1189 Angevin dynasty under Henry II
in England and France

ROMANESQUE 1000–1150

1000–1150 ROMANESQUE   GOTHIC 1150–1450

| 1075 | 1080 | 1085 | 1090 | 1095 | 1100 | 1105 | 1110 | 1115 | 1120 | 1125 | 1130 | 1135 | 1140 | 1145 | 1150 | 1155 | 1160 |

The centre nave of the cathedral

FREDERICK II, HOLY ROMAN EMPEROR

1200 Aztecs arrive in the highlands
of Mexico

1181–1226 Francis of Assisi

FROM 1215 Genghis Khan established his
Mongolian world empire

1236 Christians re-conquer
Córdoba

1165　1170　1175　1180　1185　1190　1195　1200　1205　1210　1215　1220　1225　1230　1235　1240　1245　1250

NOTRE DAME

Many older churches had to be demolished to make space for the construction of the bishop's church on the island in the Seine in Paris. After all, it was intended that in size and splendour this cathedral should surpass all the other cathedrals of France.

The King himself donated 200 livres for the new building: the cathedral would greatly increase his prestige, and he would be able to see it from his palace. However, the sum was in no way sufficient for such an ambitious project, and the man who had ordered work to begin, Bishop Maurice de Sully, had to finance the lion's share from his own coffers. Well, that's what his successor claimed. No matter how this major project was actually financed, construction began in 1163 and Notre Dame was completed about 50 years later. The dimensions were huge for the time: the building is over 130 metres (426 feet) long, and the nave is 35 metres (115 feet) high. The west front, which was begun around 1200,

is lavishly ornamented with sculptures: above the three richly decorated portals leading into the interior there is a horizontal gallery with 28 carved figures of kings, each separated from the next by a column. Above this gallery, there is a large round window. Two square towers flank the central section and are connected to each other by a series of tall, pointed arches.

The Light of God

In the 13th century, the end walls of the transepts were decorated with large rose windows; the finely decorated window on the north transept has a diameter of 13 metres (43 feet). Light is the key: the symbolism of light plays an important role not only in this cathedral, but in all Gothic cathedrals. The abbot of the St Denis Monastery to the north of Paris argued that a church should be an image of the Temple of Solomon, as described in the biblical Book of Wisdom. In this sense, the believer entering the west portal of a church could be seen as passing through the gates of Heaven into the light of God. In order to make the best use of light, large windows were necessary, and this meant piercing the

Gothic
Around the middle of the 12th century, something new developed out of the heavy forms of Romanesque architecture. Cathedrals became higher, round arches became pointed, ceilings were constructed of arched vaults supported by slender ribs, and externally buttresses were used to support the walls. These basic structural elements created a strong framework that carried the weight of the building. Now freed from this task, the walls could be pierced by windows, flooding the interior with brightly coloured light. The Gothic style, which originated in France, soon spread to England, Germany, the Netherlands, Spain and Italy, and in one form or another endured until about 1500.

NOTRE DAME, PARIS, FRANCE
From 1163

CHRONOLOGY
1163 Foundation stone laid
1177 Choir built
ca. 1200 West front completed
1240 South tower built
1250 North tower and Kings' Gallery added
13TH C Transept fronts completed
1792 Damaged extensively during the French Revolution
1843 Reconstruction begins under the direction of the architects Lassus and Viollet-le-Duc

On Quasimodo's tracks: the cathedral is the scene of Victor Hugo's historical novel *Notre Dame de Paris* (1831, *The Hunchback of Notre Dame*), which has also become famous through numerous films. The deformed bell-ringer Quasimodo observed life on the streets of medieval Paris from the top of the church's towers.

left:
View of the nave from the north with the characteristic buttresses

above:
The Blessed Mother Mary thrones above the St Anna portal

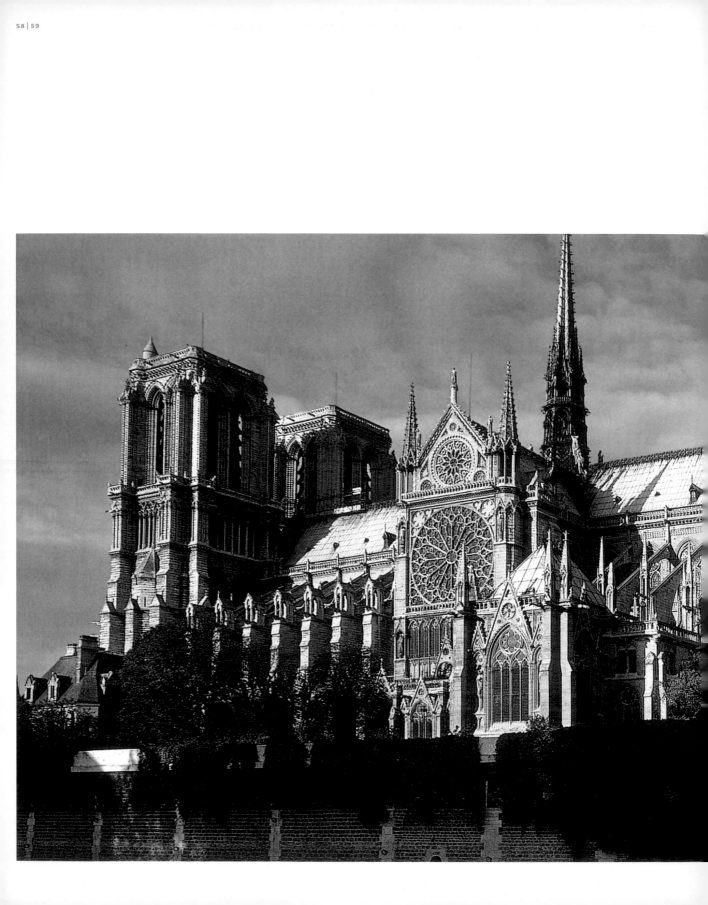

thick wall. The development of buttresses was essential in this process, for the use of external buttresses to support a building meant that it was no longer necessary for the external walls to bear the weight of the vaults and the roof. As the walls no longer had this key structural role, they could be opened up to create larger and larger windows, with the huge expanses of glass being supported by a framework of stone tracery. These windows not only allowed light to flood into the interior, they also provided an area in which biblical stories could be illustrated.

A depiction of the death of Mary is shown in the tympanum of the main portal

The façades of the transept are decorated with large rose windows

FREDERICK II, HOLY ROMAN EMPEROR

1215 *Magna Carta*, English
constitution

1206 Foundation of the Sultanate of
Delhi by Qutb al-Din Aybak

1000–1150 ROMANESQUE   GOTHIC 1150–1450

| 1140 | 1145 | 1150 | 1155 | 1160 | 1165 | 1170 | 1175 | 1180 | 1185 | 1190 | 1195 | 1200 | 1205 | 1210 | 1215 | 1220 | 1225 |

The monumental castle stands proudly
on a hill

The floor plan of the lower and upper
floors shows the repeated principle of
the number "8"

1236 Christians re-conquer Córdoba

1271 Marco Polo's departure for Asia

1241 Mongols invade Poland and Hungary

1283 Foundation of the last Mayan
capital city of Mayapán

1268 Cathedrals of Amiens

1309–1377 Pope moves
to Avignon

1230	1235	1240	1245	1250	1255	1260	1265	1270	1275	1280	1285	1290	1295	1300	1305	1310	1315

CASTEL DEL MONTE

To this day, it is still not known if its builder, Emperor Frederick II, ever actually set foot in the Castel del Monte. However, this castle in southern Italy certainly meant a lot to him, and it's reported that he was even involved in its design.

The castle, which is now shrouded in mystery, lies on a hilltop in the barren landscape of Apulia, 16 kilometres (10 miles) from the Adriatic coast. The precise date of its construction is not known, but it was probably around 1240, and it was never completed. It's hardly a castle in the real sense of the word. The building does sit on a hilltop, it's true, but it would have been difficult to defend against attack; it has neither a moat nor a drawbridge, for example. The octagonal layout of the limestone building is very unusual, and suggests that the building may have had a far from simple significance. Some of the possible uses that researchers have investigated include hunting lodge, military base, and astronomical observatory.

The Magic Number: Eight

At each of the eight corners of the octagon, there are towers, also octagonal, that are 26 metres (85 feet) high. Two sides of these towers are embedded in corners of the main tower. Small windows have been cut into the walls between the towers and those on the upper floor are decorated with Gothic tracery. The rooms are arranged on two floors around the eight-sided inner courtyard. The system of passages is carefully planned and not all rooms are directly connected with each other: visitors have to cross the courtyard several times in order to reach some of the rooms in the upper storey by way of a spiral stone staircase. The large and imposing entrance gateway on the east side of the complex clearly shows that the emperor wanted there to be no doubt about his claim to power.

Possible prototypes for the unusual Castel del Monte have been discovered in Persia and Anatolia, but the Apulian castle continues to be puzzling. Its eight sides seem to be an image of the imperial crown – one of the four that Frederick II wore. But in ancient times the octagon was also a symbol for the perfection of the cosmos; in Christianity, the number eight stands for the second coming of Christ. Or is

the tower possibly a celestial calendar in stone? At certain times of the day or year, certainly, specific shadow groupings cast by the sun and moon can be observed at the castle, and it is well known that Frederick II was interested in the natural sciences, as well as in numerology, magic, philosophy and religion. Whether the idea for Castel del Monte really can be traced back to the learned Emperor's own plans will probably always remain a mystery.

CASTEL DEL MONTE, ANDRIA, ITALY
ca. 1240

CHARACTERISTICS
Height of the main octagon 25 m/82 ft
Height of the tower 26 m/85 ft
Length of the side of the octagon
16,5 m/54 ft
Length of the sides of the tower
3,1 m/10 ft

Castel del Monte was added to the UNESCO World Heritage List in 1996.

PIERRE DE MONTREUIL, ARCHITECT

1181 Beginning of construction of
cathedral in Worms

1215 *Magna Carta*, English constitution

1220 Beginning of construction of Salisbury Cathedral

GOTHIC 1150–1450

| 1160 | 1165 | 1170 | 1175 | 1180 | 1185 | 1190 | 1195 | 1200 | 1205 | 1210 | 1215 | 1220 | 1225 | 1230 | 1235 | 1240 | 1245 |

Westminster Abbey with the west-tower
façade, seen from the south

1248 Beginning of construction of the Alhambra in Granada

1278 Greatest expanse of the Mongol Empire under Kublai Khan

1255–1319 Duccio di Buoninsegna

1295 Arnolfo di Cambio begins the cathedral of Santa Maria del Fiore, Florence

1328 England recognizes Scottish independence

| 1250 | 1255 | 1260 | 1265 | 1270 | 1275 | 1280 | 1285 | 1290 | 1295 | 1300 | 1305 | 1310 | 1315 | 1320 | 1325 | 1330 | 1335 |

WESTMINSTER ABBEY

In 1245, King Henry III ordered work to begin on the royal abbey church of Westminster; it would take several centuries to complete. The result was the tallest church in England, its nave reaching the imposing height of 32 metres (105 feet) – a church grand enough to be the setting for royal ceremonies to this day.

With Westminster Abbey, many of the characteristics of French Gothic architecture made their way to the centre of London. That's no surprise, for the church's first master builder was a certain Henry de Reyns (Henry of Reims) – the influence of the architects and stonemasons who were active in Reims in northern France spread to many European countries. This is why, for example, the choir in Westminster is adorned with an ambulatory with radiating chapels, similar to those in French cathedrals. The high windows of Westminster Abbey are supported by an elaborate stone tracery in what is known as the Decorated Style, which made its way across England over the next hundred years. It's named after the lavish decoration that can be found on all parts of the building: the walls and ceiling, the pillars and buttresses, overflow with ornaments.

Gothic Old and New

At the beginning of the 16th century, Henry VI enhanced the east end of the church with a superb chapel, the walls of which are decorated with 95 statues of saints. The most impressive aspect of this chapel is, however, the ceiling, which is covered with fan vaulting. This intricate ceiling structure, with its slender ribs spreading out in a fan shape, was completed in 1509. Fan vaulting of this kind, which is characteristic of the English late medieval period, is described as being in the Perpendicular Style. Two centuries were to pass before the west front of the abbey was given its present appearance. The two flanking towers were not completed until the 18th century, so that here the tracery windows are in a style far more restrained than are those in the much earlier eastern sections of the building.

Princes and the Famous

To this day, the abbey church of Westminster has retained its civic importance. William the Conqueror was crowned in the abbey that stood there before the present one, and since then Westminster has established itself as the site of the coronations and funerals of the English kings and queens. Many other important personalities, including the composer George Frederick Handel and the scientist Isaac Newton, are also buried in the abbey church. One of the most visited of the 3,000 graves in the Abbey is that of the Unknown Soldier, erected in memory of the fallen of the First World War.

WESTMINSTER ABBEY, LONDON, ENGLAND
From 1245

CHRONOLOGY
ca. 960 Original Benedictine abbey founded
A stone building erected to replace the old abbey church
1065 St Peter's Church (Westminster) consecrated
1066 William the Conqueror crowned in the abbey
FROM 1245 Henry III has the church reconstructed in the Gothic style
EARLY 16TH C Henry VII commissions the construction of the chapel at the end of the choir
18TH C West tower front completed following plans by Nicholas Hawksmoor; the west window and rosette window are created

Westminster Abbey can be visited online at:
http://www.westminster-abbey.org/

left:
The palmette-like ribbed vault spans the central nave

above:
The west façade of the church

PIERRE DE MONTREUIL, ARCHITECT

ARNOLFO DI CAMBIO, ARCHITECT

1220 Beginning of construction of Salisbury Cathedral

1248 Beginning of construction of the Alhambra in Granada

1215 *Magna Carta*, English constitution

1255–1319 Duccio di Buoninsegna

GOTHIC 1150–1450

| 1180 | 1185 | 1190 | 1195 | 1200 | 1205 | 1210 | 1215 | 1220 | 1225 | 1230 | 1235 | 1240 | 1245 | 1250 | 1255 | 1260 | 1265 |

The Halls of Harmony on a three-tiered terrace

right:
The throne in the Hall of the Preservation of Harmony

1271 Marco Polo becomes the Mongol
Great Khan's governor

1278 Greatest expanse of the Mongol
Empire under Kublai Khan

1314 Construction of the Palazzo Vecchio
in Florence

1328 England recognizes Scottish independence

| 1270 | 1275 | 1280 | 1285 | 1290 | 1295 | 1300 | 1305 | 1310 | 1315 | 1320 | 1325 | 1330 | 1335 | 1340 | 1345 | 1350 | 1355 |

THE FORBIDDEN CITY

In building this extraordinary royal palace, the emperors of China were creating a self-contained royal universe remote from the real world. Work began at the beginning of the 15th century, and for the following five centuries it was the only world they knew. Little is known about the builders of the gigantic complex, but the accounts of the highly ritualised life at the Chinese court still fascinate us today.

The "crimson" imperial palace gets its name from the red buildings and walls that surround the enormous area. Between 1406 and 1421, around 200,000 workers toiled to build the innumerable palaces and pavilions, gates and gardens, on a site that measures an astonishing 720,000 square metres (7,750,000 square feet). The Chinese believed that the Forbidden City was not only the centre of the Empire, but also the centre of the universe.

A City within a City

The main axis of the palace complex runs from south to north, the Meridian Gate in the south being the main entrance to the palace district. The size of the gate caused the members of a 17th-century Dutch delegation to think that they were standing in front of the entire palace, but in fact they had seen only a fraction of the complex, which has a total of 8,886 rooms. The Meridian Gate leads directly into the government quarters, which could be entered only by ministers, officials and the military. The Golden River, which winds its way through this section of the palace under five marble bridges, represents the five virtues of Confucianism: humanity, honesty, dignity, wisdom and reverence.

A three-tiered terrace leads from a square, which measures 200 x 190 metres (656 x 623 feet), to the Hall of Supreme Harmony. The size of this hall eclipses that of all of the other buildings in the Forbidden City, and no building inside or outside the palace walls was allowed to be taller than its 34-metre (112-feet) Throne Hall. The Emperor held his major audience there three times a year. Dragons, the symbols of his power, can be seen throughout the palace complex.

Strict Protocol

Between 1421 and 1924, 24 emperors and their courts lived behind the high walls, further separated from the common people by a wide moat. The living quarters of the imperial family were located in the northern sector of the complex. And not only they had to be accommodated there: as many as 9,000 ladies-in-waiting, 20,000 eunuchs and 5,000 guards are listed in the court archives as having lived in the palace area. Every step they took was precisely predetermined and the use of the various paths through the complex strictly regulated. Ministers and eunuchs had to approach the Emperor and Empress on their knees, his wives could see the Emperor only by official appointment, and the imperial children were always accompanied by whole processions of servants. They would have been very sorry indeed if one of the imperial children took off and disappeared into the imperial gardens!

THE FORBIDDEN CITY, BEIJING, CHINA
1406–21

FACT FILE
Area 720,000 sq m/7,750,000 sq ft
Constructed area 150,000 sq m/
1,614,585 sq ft
Number of palaces 890
Number of rooms 8,886
Use Imperial palace until 1924;
today, the Palace Museum

In 1986 and 1987, the Forbidden City served as the location for Bernardo Bertolucci's sumptuous film *The Last Emperor*. The interactive map at http://www.chinavista.com/beijing/gugong/!start.html gives an impression of the size and layout of the Forbidden City as well as photographs and information on its history.

1	Gate of Divine Prowess
2	Hall of Imperial Peace
3	Imperial Garden
4	Gate of Earthly Peace
5	Six Western Palaces
6	Palace of Earthly Peace
7	Hall of Union
8	Palace of Heavenly Purity
9	Palace of the Culture of the Mind
10	Gate of Heavenly Purity
11	Palace of Peaceful Old Age
12	Hall of the Preservation of Harmony
13	Hall of Perfect Harmony
14	Hall of Supreme Harmony
15	Gate of Supreme Harmony
16	Meridian Gate

The Imperial Palace – A view of the
Forbidden City at sunrise

1250 Democratic constitution in Florence

1268 End of German Imperial rule in Italy

1271 Marco Polo became governor
of the Mongol Empire

1307 Dante Alighieri begins the *Divine Comedy*

1314 Construction of the Palazzo
Vecchio in Florence

GOTHIC 1150–1450

| 1240 | 1245 | 1250 | 1255 | 1260 | 1265 | 1270 | 1275 | 1280 | 1285 | 1290 | 1295 | 1300 | 1305 | 1310 | 1315 | 1320 | 1325 |

The Doge's Palace on the lagoon

1355 Charles IV, Holy Roman Emperor

1381 Venetian supremacy in the Mediterranean
following victory over Genoa

| 1330 | 1335 | 1340 | 1345 | 1350 | 1355 | 1360 | 1365 | 1370 | 1375 | 1380 | 1385 | 1390 | 1395 | 1400 | 1405 | 1410 | 1415 |

THE DOGE'S PALACE

By the 14th century, more room was needed to house the councillors who governed Venice from the Maggior Consiglio. As their number had risen to 1,800, the former building had become far too small. So, in 1340, the foundation stone of a new seat of government was laid, alongside the Grand Canal.

The new meeting room for the city councillors, measuring 54 x 25 metres (177 x 82 feet), was in keeping with the increased demands on space. And, as was the case with all the richly decorated rooms in the Doge's Palace, it was also a place for grand receptions and ceremonies. Paintings by the great Venetian masters, set in elaborate gilded frames, graced the walls and ceilings.

A Naval Power Holds Court

Construction of the palace was to continue into the 17th century. Initially, the west wing was renovated under Doge Francesco Foscari. He had the Porta della Carta built in the north of the palace to provide a connection with St Mark's basilica, and the east wing was added after the fire of 1483, completing the U-form layout of three buildings grouped around an inner courtyard.

The façade of the Doge's Palace is characterized above all by the contrast between the two lower floors, which open outwards as loggias carried by delicate columns and keel arches broken with tracery, and the upper floor, which – with the exception of the lancet windows – is completely covered with red and white marble. Venice's adoption of Gothic was determined by its links with the East as well as the West. By the 15th century, the city on the lagoon had become a major marine and trading power, and had particularly close links with the East: influences from the Byzantine Empire had been seen there for a long time. Symbols of Venice's former power on land and sea can be clearly seen in the Doge's Palace: the staircase in the inner courtyard is flanked by two monumental statues of the gods Neptune (sea) and Mars (war).

From the Paper Gateway to the Bridge of Sighs

The impressive size of the Porta della Carta (Paper Gateway), which forms the main entrance to the Doge's Palace, was in keeping with the rich decoration and status of the building. Giovanni and Bartolomeo Bon were commissioned its creation. High above the entrance stands the Lion of St Mark, in front of which kneels Doge Foscari. A window decorated with tracery rises above this and the gateway ends in a pediment. Sculptures representing the virtues, columns and small knob-like applications decorate the ensemble. The "Paper Gateway" is a surprising name for such a magnificent and important portal. It stems from the fact that petitioners could bring their appeals, written on paper, only as far as this gateway: they were not allowed to enter the palace. The name of the nearby Ponte dei Sospiri (Bridge of Sighs) also hardly seems appropriate for its grand surroundings, until its purpose is understood – it forms the only link to the neighbouring building on the east side of the palace, a prison erected in the 16th century.

THE DOGE'S PALACE, VENICE, ITALY
From 1340

CHRONOLOGY
1340 Foundation stone of the new Doge's Palace laid
FIRST HALF 15TH C West wing added
1438–42 Giovanni and Bartolomeo Bon build the Porta della Carta
FROM 1483 East wing built
1559 Palace completed
1577 A fire destroys a major part of the palace's pictorial decoration
SECOND HALF 16TH C New prison built
1797 End of the Venetian Republic
1811–1904 The Biblioteca Marciana housed in the Doge's Palace
LATE 19TH C Extensive restoration work undertaken
SINCE 1996 The Doge's Palace is now part of a museum, the Musei Civici Veneziani

St Mark's Square; detail of a painting by G. B. Arzenti

Delicate columns and tracery arches
characterize the two lower storeys while
the upper storey is covered with marble

The Porta della Carta, main entrance
to the Doge's Palace

SIGISMUND OF LUXEMBOURG, HOLY ROMAN EMPEROR

FREDERICK III, HOLY ROMAN EMPEROR

1347 Devastating plague epidemic in Europe

1378 Vatican becomes papal residence

1355 Charles IV becomes Holy Roman Emperor

ca. 1412 Discovery of the linear perspective by Brunelleschi

| 1330 | 1335 | 1340 | 1345 | 1350 | 1355 | 1360 | 1365 | 1370 | 1375 | 1380 | 1385 | 1390 | 1395 | 1400 | 1405 | 1410 | 1415 |

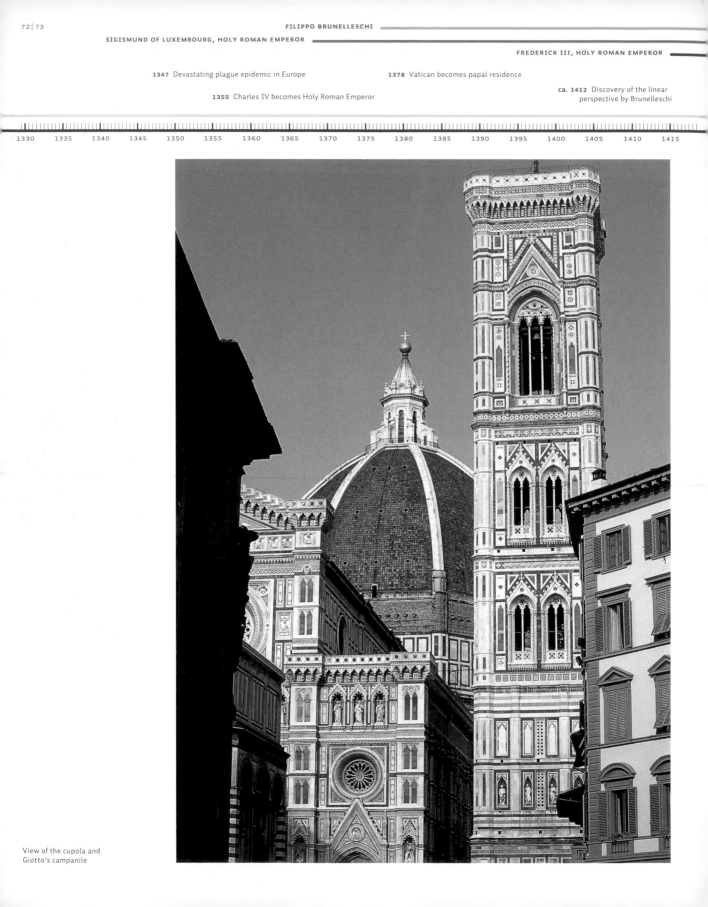

View of the cupola and Giotto's campanile

1434–1464 Cosimo de' Medici
rules in Florence

1453 Conquest of Constantinople
by the Turks

1469–1492 Lorenzo de' Medici
rules in Florence

1492 Start of Columbus' voyages
of discovery to America

1150–1450 GOTHIC   EARLY RENAISSANCE 1450–1500

1450–1500 EARLY RENAISSANCE

1420   1425   1430   1435   1440   1445   1450   1455   1460   1465   1470   1475   1480   1485   1490   1495   1500   1505

CATHEDRAL DOME IN FLORENCE

In 1418 there was a competition to find a design for the dome of Florence Cathedral. It attracted several artists and architects, for it was a major project, and finally the plans by Filippo Brunelleschi were accepted. In the decades that followed, he performed a superb technical feat in building the dome, though it was an achievement not recognised by those who had commissioned him.

The building of Florence Cathedral, Santa Maria del Fiore, in the centre of Florence, was making steady progress, but the dome was still to be tackled. And the Florentines wanted something very special: the octagonal drum, the lower section of the dome construction, measures a handsome 45 metres (148 feet) in diameter, so the dome would have to be huge. It was a truly ambitious project: their dome was to be larger that the one that graced the ancient Pantheon in Rome. This spirit of competition was driven not only by a desire to surpass antiquity, but also by the ambition of the important Florentine guilds. The Arte della Lana, the rich wool-workers' guild, was in charge of the construction of the cathedral and they quite clearly wanted to erect a monument that reflected well on them.

Problems Big and Small

With their decision to employ Filippo Brunelleschi, the selection committee had chosen a very experienced master builder. However, they remained sceptical, and gave him control of construction only up to a specific height. Brunelleschi accepted this limitation with fortitude and got down to work. And it was difficult. He was confronted with different problems every day: how, for example, could he get the enor-

mously heavy building materials, sandstone and marble, up to the dizzy heights where they were needed? In response, he invented lifting hoists that were driven by oxen, hoists that had both forward and reverse gears. And so that the workers didn't have to go though the tiring climb down from – and back up to – the dome at midday, he had kitchens and wine store installed under the roof of the church. His main concern, however, was the construction of the dome itself. This, ingeniously, he built in two layers: the inner one carries structural weight, the external provides protection from the weather. This "hollow" design enabled Brunelleschi to reduce the total weight of the vast dome.

Late Recognition

But the members of Arte della Lana were still not convinced. Quite the opposite, in fact. In 1432, when time was drawing near to commission the lantern to crown the dome, they once again organized a competition, and it was only four years later that they were prepared to accept Brunelleschi's model for this final phase of construction. In the meantime, the architect had been harassed by his opponents. He was even thrown into prison for two weeks for working as a builder without belonging to the stonemasons' guild. It was not until after his death in 1446 that the people of Florence recognized his genius and honoured the great architect with a tomb in the heart of the cathedral. His memorial reads: "Here lies the body of a man of great inventiveness, Filippo Brunelleschi of Florence."

CATHEDRAL DOME, FLORENCE, ITALY
1418–36 (Cupola)

Filippo Brunelleschi

1377 Born in Florence
1404 Becomes member of the Florentine Goldsmiths' Guild
1401 Takes part in the competition for the decoration of the door of the Florentine baptistery
1418 Wins competition for the design of the cathedral dome
1419–24 Ospedale degli Innocenti orphanage in Florence
1420 Starts work on the cathedral dome
1420s Old sacristy of San Lorenzo and the Pazzi Chapel, Santa Croce, both in Florence
1436 Commissioned to design a lantern for the cathedral's dome
1446 Dies 16 April in Florence

> ## Renaissance
> The Italian 16th-century art historian Giorgio Vasari was the first to speak of a Rinascimento – a "rebirth" or Renaissance – of the arts. For him, this was the flowering of art after what he saw as the gloom of the Middle Ages. The term Renaissance is now used to describe the era's painting, sculpture, architecture, philosophy and literature. It was a culture characterized by a return to the works of antiquity, a passion for perspective, and, last but not least, a completely new understanding of man as the summit of creation. The Italian Renaissance had its origins in 15th-century Florence.

The cathedral with its massive cupola
dominates the townscape of Florence

ca. **1412** Discovery of the linear
perspective by Brunelleschi

ca. **1455** Invention of book printing, Gutenberg

1150–1450 GOTHIC   EARLY RENAISSANCE 1450–1500

| 1400 | 1405 | 1410 | 1415 | 1420 | 1425 | 1430 | 1435 | 1440 | 1445 | 1450 | 1455 | 1460 | 1465 | 1470 | 1475 | 1480 | 1485 |

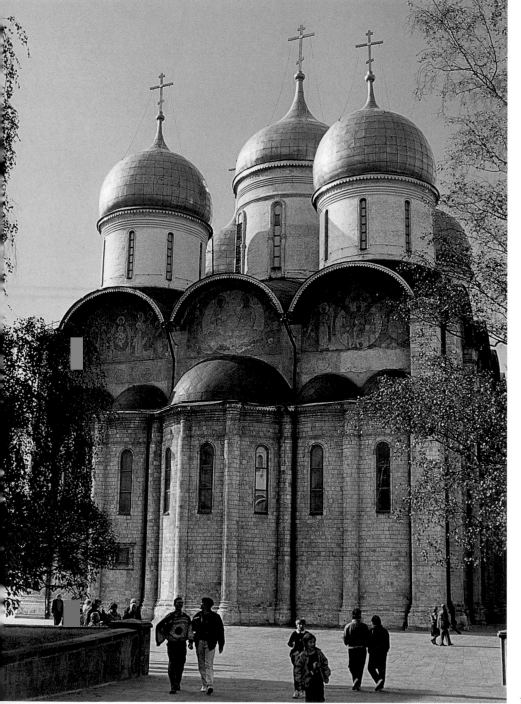

The Dormition Cathedral in the Kremlin

IVAN IV VASILYEVICH, FIRST TSAR OF RUSSIA

1517 Beginning of the Reformation (Luther's theses)

1520/21 Magellan's circumnavigation of the globe

1508–1512 Beginning of work on the frescoes in the Sistine Chapel, Michelangelo

1541 Spain conquers the Mayan empire in Central America

1571 Naval battle at Lepanto: Italian and Spanish fleets end Turkish maritime domination

1529 Turks besiege Vienna

1450–1500 EARLY RENAISSANCE   HIGH RENAISSANCE 1500–1550

1500–1550 HIGH RENAISSANCE   LATE RENAISSANCE 1550–1600

1490   1495   1500   1505   1510   1515   1520   1525   1530   1535   1540   1545   1550   1555   1560   1565   1570   1575

THE KREMLIN

Walls, ramparts and towers are the characteristics of a kremlin, the fortified section of a Russian city. However, the example in Moscow, which was constructed from the 14th to the 19th century, is very special: with its palaces and cathedrals it has remained a symbol of Russia's power to this day. It is now a fine museum.

This former seat of the Russian princes from the 12th century is older than the country it serves today as a political and cultural heart. After 1485, Ivan III speeded up the conversion of the site into a fortified city. He selected Italian architects, who initially devoted themselves to the Kremlin's defence system. Since that time, 2,235 metres (7,330 feet) of a red brick wall, laid out in the form of a triangle, were built around this raised area in the centre of Moscow. Twenty towers, each of them differently decorated, are inserted into the surrounding wall. The main entrance is in the highest of them, the Trinity Tower, on the west side. However, statesmen enter through the Redeemer Tower Gate immediately in front of the government buildings in the north-east of the Kremlin. This tower gets its name from the icon of the Redeemer which originally hung above the gate, and which religious processions filed past. The Arsenal Tower, erected on the massive walls at the northern corner of the Kremlin, is strategically important: the wells in its cellar guaranteed the supply of water in times of siege, and even had a secret passageway that allowed those besieged to leave the Kremlin unseen.

Church Domes and Palaces

The heart of the 28-hectare (70-acre) complex is the rectangular Cathedral Square. In addition to five churches and four palaces, the square boasts an 81-meter (266-feet) tall bell tower from where the largest bell in the world tolled in the 18th century. The bell's 200,000 kilos (nearly 200 tons) of metal, distributed over a diameter of 6.5 metres (21 feet), was shattered following a fall only a few years after its installation. The Kremlin palaces have also been ravaged by time; the largest building had to be reconstructed in the 19th century, and a great number of historical styles were resorted to. The old seat of the tsars, the Terem Palace (erected in 1635/36) can still be admired in all its old glory. Its five

storeys are crowned with eleven golden domes that rest on bases covered in green tiles.

The Dormition Cathedral is less playful but considerably more impressive. The tsars passed through the richly decorated south portal to enter their coronation church. Its counterpart is the Church of the Annunciation on the south-west of the square. The many new domes on the former churches of the tsars were an expression of their increasing wealth. After the Russian Revolution, they became museums. However, there is an old Russian saying, "The Kremlins is above the city, but only God is above the Kremlin" – and now religious services are again held in the cathedrals.

THE KREMLIN, MOSCOW, RUSSIA
From 1156

CHRONOLOGY
1156 Start of fortification works
1386 First cathedral built inside the Kremlin
1485–1516 Kremlin extended: enclosed within a brick wall, the Faceted Palace, the Archangel and Dormition cathedrals built
1547 Ivan IV is the first Tsar to be crowned in the Kremlin
17TH C Poteshny (Amusement) Palace, Terem Palace and the Cathedral of Twelve Apostles added
1712 Tsar moves his court to St Petersburg
1806 First museum building constructed within the Kremlin
1814 First Kremlin museum opened
1844–51 The Armoury, Russia's treasury, constructed
1918 Lenin orders the return of the government from St Petersburg to the Kremlin
1961 Congress Palace erected
1955 Kremlin (partially) opened for visitors

The Kremlin and its museums are open daily, except on Thursdays, from 10am to 5pm. Additional information on the history and possibilities for visiting the Kremlin can be found on the website: http://www.kremlin.ru/eng/

The Kremlin houses palaces
and cathedrals

St Peter's Basilica is crowned by the cupola designed by Michelangelo

IVAN IV VASILYEVICH,
FIRST TSAR OF RUSSIA   **1529** Turks besiege Vienna

1519 Charles V, Holy Roman Emperor   **1546** Peak of the Fugger's financial power,
                                                        with wealth valued at 4 million gulden
1517 Beginning of the Reformation (Luther's theses)   **1588** Sinking of the
1512–1514 *Sistine Madonna*, Raphael   Spanish Armada

                          1500–1550 HIGH RENAISSANCE   LATE RENAISSANCE 1550–1600

1510   1515   1520   1525   1530   1535   1540   1545   1550   1555   1560   1565   1570   1575   1580   1585   1590   1595

ST PETER'S BASILICA

The list of builders who worked on St Peter's in Rome reads like a "who's who" of 16th-century architects. For over a century, this important pilgrimage church, the largest sacred building in Christendom, was designed and redesigned, its many plans redrawn and then discarded ... until, finally, the new St Peter's came into being — a building that embraces the Renaissance, Mannerism and finally the Baroque.

At the end of the 16th century, Rome was immensely powerful in both the political and cultural spheres. One clear indication of this can be found in the radical urban planning that the Renaissance popes pursued. Streets were laid out, palaces, churches and fountains built, and the Vatican became a major part of the city centre. The most prestigious project of all was St Peter's, which was built above the grave of the Apostle St Peter.

Papal Ambitions
The old St Peter's, the predecessor of today's church, looked back on a history of more than a thousand years, and it was in poor condition. In time, it was also too small. The first plans for the construction of a new Vatican church had already been drawn up in the 15th century. However, it was Pope Julius II who declared that the new St Peter's would finally be built. He was a Pope entirely devoted to supporting the arts – and to ensuring that his fame endured in the form of

impressive monuments. In April 1506, Julius had the foundation stone of the new building laid. The architect Donato Bramante had provided the plans: a gigantic central-plan construction in the form of a Greek cross (with four arms of equal length) was envisaged. Later, the architect added a nave to create more space for the congregation, so that the building took on the more traditional form of a church. Julius had announced a special papal indulgence to finance the gigantic project, but the papal plans far exceeded penitents' willingness to donate. When Bramante died in 1514, work on most of the sections had barely begun; in fact, only the choir had progressed. Raphael, Sangallo and, later, Peruzzi were the next architects in charge of construction. Raphael planed a longitudinal layout upon a Latin cross. However, progress was again slow. Luther's attack on the trade in indulgences had important consequences for the new St Peter's: financing their project became even more difficult.

A Baroque Conclusion
It was only when Pope Paul III commissioned Michelangelo with the task of completing St Peter's that work quickened and the basilica finally started to take shape. A huge dome finally crowned the church, which in its size and grandeur would symbolize the growing power and confidence of Catholicism after the Reformation.

In the middle of the 17th century, St Peter's Square, in front of the cathedral, was given its present appearance by the architect and sculptor Lorenzo Bernini. Two ovals in succession, both bordered by rows of huge columns, frame the Baroque façade of St Peter's, designed by Carlo Maderno, and heighten the overwhelming impact of the building.

**ST PETER'S BASILICA,
VATICAN CITY, ROME, ITALY**
From 1506

CHRONOLOGY
1506 Foundation stone for the new construction is laid
1514 Chief architect Donato Bramante dies. Raphael is the next builder, followed by Antonio da Sangallo the Younger and Baldassare Peruzzi
1547 Michelangelo takes over the supervision of construction
ca. 1588 Giacomo della Porta and Domenico Fontana complete the dome designed by Michelangelo
1607–14 Carlo Maderno builds the nave and west front
1624 Bernini erects the monumental bronze baldachin over the grave of St Peter
1626 St Peter's basilica consecrated
MID 17TH C Bernini adds the colonnades on St Peter's Square

The Baroque façade of St Peter's Basilica
with the famous central loggia

below:
Bernini's monumental bronze baldachin
rises above the grave of St Peter

ca. 1455 Gutenberg Bible	**1472** First printing of Dante's *Divine Comedy*	**1510** *Garden of Earthly Delights*, Hieronymus Bosch
		1506 Beginning of the new St Peter's, Rome

1150–1450 GOTHIC   EARLY RENAISSANCE 1450–1500   1450–1500 EARLY RENAISSANCE   HIGH RENAISSANCE 1500–1550

1425 1430 1435 1440 1445 1450 1455 1460 1465 1470 1475 1480 1485 1490 1495 1500 1505 1510

King Francis I's hunting lodge –
"utopia turned to stone"

Floor plan of the castle from 1576

1529 Turks besiege Vienna

1514 Niccolò Machiavelli's *The Prince*

1562 Huguenot Wars in France

ca. 1588 Completion of
St Peter's dome following
plans by Michelangelo

1500–1550 HIGH RENAISSANCE   LATE RENAISSANCE 1550–1600

1550–1600 LATE RENAISSANCE

1515   1520   1525   1530   1535   1540   1545   1550   1555   1560   1565   1570   1575   1580   1585   1590   1595   1600

CHÂTEAU OF CHAMBORD

The French king Francis I had recently suffered a political defeat. In 1519, not he but the Hapsburg Charles V had been elected Emperor of the Holy Roman Empire. A fact that at least settled, for the moment, the struggle for European supremacy.

However, this didn't mean that Francis could sit back – there was a need to extend and consolidate his power in France. So at the end of 1519, construction began on a grand royal château in the Loire Valley, where the court and nobility had settled. Francis had a wall built around a 5,500-hectare (13,560-acre) park and woodland, and in the centre of this royal hunting domain he built the Château of Chambord.

"A Utopia in Stone"

This was Prince Metternich's much later description of Chambord. Francis I was particularly fond of contemporary Italian art and architecture and brought many artists from Italy to his court. So it's not surprising that Italian as well as French elements can also be seen in the construction of this "hunting lodge", a description that hardly reflects the château's size and magnificence.

Chambord rises above a base measuring 156 x 117 metres (512 x 304 feet), with the prominent central section being on the north-west side. Similar to the donjons of mediaeval castles, this section stressed the fortress-like character of the château. The central tower is surrounded by three-storied side wings;

Château Construction

Monumental dimensions are by no means unusual for châteaux. These seats of the nobility, which in the 15th century replaced castles as the residences of the aristocracy, were often built as an enclosed group of buildings arranged around a central courtyard. They are frequently also open on one side so that three wings form an imposing reception court known as a "court of honour." The main façades are characterised by pavilions, usually on the corners, and by projections that jut out in the centre or on the sides. In the 17th and 18th centuries, known as the Age of Absolutism, châteaux played a major role is displaying power and wealth.

the additional wings were built only to the ground floor level. Four massive round towers are meant to create the impression that the château is well defended. The wide garden at the front of the château, as so often in French grand houses, is set out in strict geometrical order. The extraordinary double spiral staircase, which was completed in 1530, was inspired by Mannerism, a style noted for its use of the irrational or extravagant.

The plans for Chambord probably originated with the Italian Domenico da Cortona, though Jacques and Denis Sourdeau were among the French architects involved in the construction. One other name is connected with the largest of all the Loire châteaux – that of the inventor and artist Leonardo da Vinci: he spent the last years of his life as a guest of Francis I at Amboise, not far away, and it has been suggested that he may have had a hand in the design of Chambord.

Gothic Echoes

Emperor Charles V was enthusiastic when he visited Chambord in 1539; he felt the château to be "the epitome of what human art is capable of achieving". However, at the time, construction had not been completed. In fact, the largest Loire château was never completed, though even in this "unfinished" state it has 440 rooms. The layout was in keeping with contemporary ideas of comfort: the rooms were not arranged in suites but divided into independent, three-room apartments. It is more likely that the Emperor was fascinated above all by the remarkable skyline rather than the interior. There are 365 chimneys, around 800 small turrets, bell towers and oriels rising up from the roofs of Chambord. Reminiscent of the small pointed towers of Gothic cathedrals, these towers and chimneys create a strong impression of a city in miniature.

CHÂTEAU OF CHAMBORD, FRANCE
From 1519

FACT FILE
Location 320 k/200 miles SW of Paris
Builder Francis I (1494–1547)
Area of the park 5,440 hectares/
  21 sq miles
Number of rooms More than 400
Number of staircases 84
Owner The state, since 1932
1981 UNESCO World Heritage Site
Visitors per year Approx. 800,000

The château and park of Chambord can be visited daily – also online, at http://www.chambord.org/educ/libre-GB.htm

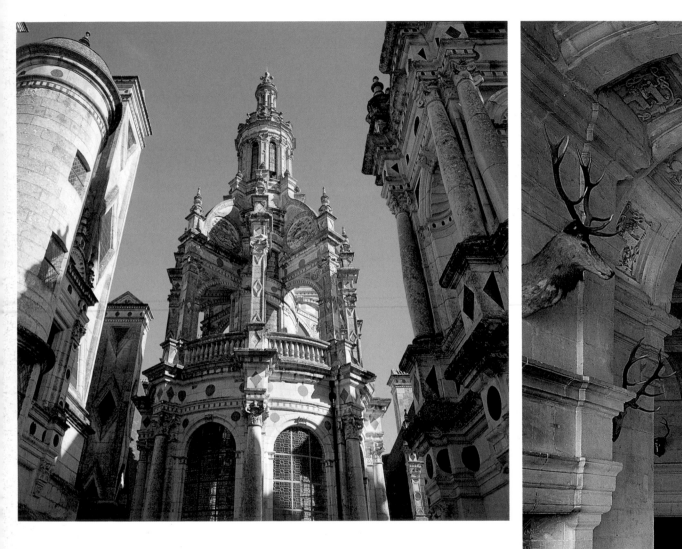

above:
Detail of the bizarre roof landscape

right:
Staircase, with its double spiral course,
in the centre of the main building

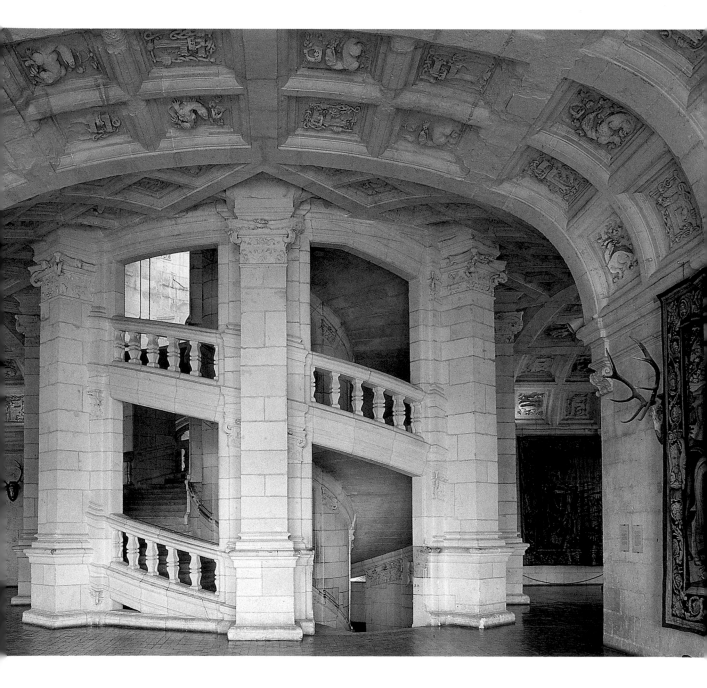

1438–1527 Peak period of the Inca kingdom

ca. 1455 Invention of book printing, Gutenberg

1476 Greatest expanse of the Chimú realm in South America

1150–1450 GOTHIC   EARLY RENAISSANCE 1450–1500

1450–1500 EARLY RENAISSANCE   HIGH RENAISSANCE 1500–1550

1425   1430   1435   1440   1445   1450   1455   1460   1465   1470   1475   1480   1485   1490   1495   1500   1505   1510

Stone witnesses to the past:
the ruins of the Inca city

below:
Located high in the Peruvian Andes:
Machu Picchu

1517 Beginning of the Reformation (Luther's theses)

1512–1514 *Sistine Madonna*, Raphael   **1532** Spain begins the conquest of the Inca kingdom

1529 Turks besiege Vienna

ca. 1588 Completion of
St Peter's dome following
plans by Michelangelo

1500–1550 HIGH RENAISSANCE   LATE RENAISSANCE 1550–1600

1550–1600 LATE RENAISSANCE

1515 1520 1525 1530 1535 1540 1545 1550 1555 1560 1565 1570 1575 1580 1585 1590 1595 1600

MACHU PICCHU

The expedition led by the American adventurer Hiram Bingham (probably the original Indiana Jones) had actually set off to the Peruvian Andes in the hope of finding the mysterious Inca city of Vilcamba. What they discovered in summer 1911 proved to be no less sensational.

Three days' march from the old Inca capital city of Cuzco, the group came across ruins overgrown with dense jungle. Could it be Vilcamba? Bingham was convinced it was, and in the following years he had the settlement on the rocky plateau fully excavated. What he'd found became world famous when the National Geographic magazine devoted its entire April 1913 edition to it. The final realisation that it was not Vilcamba did not dampen enthusiasm. What Bingham had really found was even more remarkable: the lost Inca city of Machu Picchu.

Hidden in the Mountains

The Inca probably founded this settlement, which is perched on a mountainside a good 2,300 metres (7,550 feet) above sea level, around the middle of the 15th century. Its purpose and history are shrouded in mystery and very few specific dates are known. According to one theory, Machu Picchu was the residence of the Inca ruler Pachacútec, who settled there with his court and introduced the cult of the sun god Inti. Another theory argues that astronomic calculations were carried out at Machu Picchu. No single explanation is universally accepted.

It seems likely that the complex was probably still under construction a hundred years later when the Spanish conquered the country. Unlike other Inca settlements, however, Machu Picchu remained hidden in the mountains and the city was never looted. However, for some reason the indigenous population abandoned Machu Picchu, taking all their possessions with them.

Terraces and Panoramic Views

More than 200 houses, set in neat rows, have been preserved in Machu Picchu. They were originally connected to each other by a series of narrow streets, pathways and flights of steps. The surrounding land was terraced for agriculture. However, the silos for storing foodstuffs, typical of Inca cities, are missing. Nevertheless, there can be doubt

that people had settled there, for the Machu Picchu complex was clearly divided into a residential area and a temple area. In fact, it's been estimated that approximately 1,000 people could have lived in the city. Some found their final resting place there: since the first expedition, 50 burial sites have been found. The Inca built their living quarters, temples and workshops out of large stones so precisely hewn that they were able to do without mortar. The transport of the huge stones from a nearby quarry was, in itself, another astonishing achievement.

MACHU PICCHU, PERU
Start of construction 15th C

CHRONOLOGY
15TH C Probable beginning of the Machu Picchu complex
ca. 1520 The Inca kingdom reaches it greatest expanse
1533 Pizzarro takes the city of Cuzco
1782 Official record of the sale of Machu Picchu and the surrounding land made
1895 A route from Cuzco to Machu Picchu established
1911 Academic and explorer Hiram Bingham discovers the ruins of Machu Picchu
1912/13 Bingham starts excavations
1983 UNESCO World Heritage Site

Through the Internet site http://www.destination360.com/peru/machu-picchu.php it's possible to make a virtual visit to the natural and cultural monument of Machu Picchu.

The Inca Emperor Atahualpa and his realm

1532 Spain begins the conquest of the Inca kingdom

1526 Beginning of the Mogul Empire in India

1450–1500 EARLY RENAISSANCE   HIGH RENAISSANCE 1500–1550   1500–1550 HIGH RENAISSANCE   LATE RENAISSANCE 1550–1600

| 1480 | 1485 | 1490 | 1495 | 1500 | 1505 | 1510 | 1515 | 1520 | 1525 | 1530 | 1535 | 1540 | 1545 | 1550 | 1555 | 1560 | 1565 |

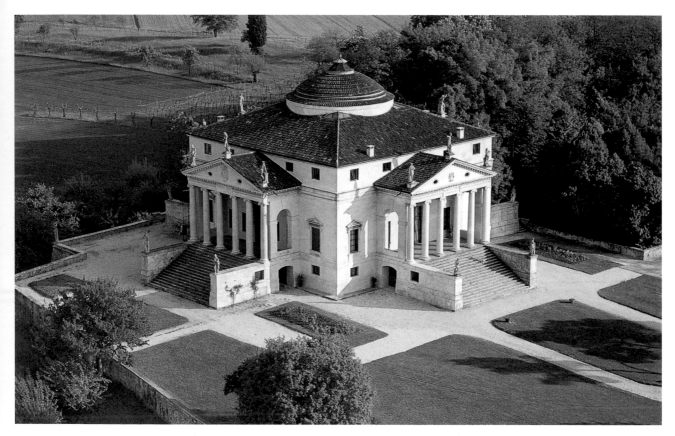

Perfect proportions: The Villa la Rotonda
near Vicenza

below:
Andrea Palladio, floor plan und cross-
section, woodcut from *I Quattro Libri
dell'Architettura*, 1570

Palladianism

Palladio's architecture found many admirers in
the following centuries. Inigo Jones imported the
Italian architect's theories into England, and
many builders in the Netherlands, Scandinavia
and Germany were inspired by his country villas
and also by his architectural writings. In the 18th
century, private houses and public buildings were
often modelled on Palladian country villas. When
planning his country home Monticello in Virginia,
the American President Thomas Jefferson
followed the style of Palladio's Villa la Rotonda
closely (see pages 110–111).

1602 The Dutch found the Cape Colony in South Africa

ca. 1588 Completion of St Peter's
dome following plans
by Michelangelo

1607 First English colony in America, Virginia

1618–1648 Thirty Years' War

1632 Beginning of construction of the Taj Mahal, India

1639 English settlement in Madras
(India), later the seat of the
East-India Trading Company

1550–1600 LATE RENAISSANCE BAROQUE 1600–1730

1570 1575 1580 1585 1590 1595 1600 1605 1610 1615 1620 1625 1630 1635 1640 1645 1650 1655

VILLA LA ROTONDA

In the 16th century, there was scarcely a well-to-do Venetian who didn't want a villa on the mainland. This region, known as the Veneto, was not just a place to relax away from the hubbub of crowded Venice: the fertile land of the Veneto provided Venice with most of its food, and so the fine houses there were often linked with farms.

It was therefore necessary to take the demands of agriculture into consideration when planning villas. Even Andrea Palladio, the most famous villa architect in the Veneto region, included them in his designs. He was inspired above all by the villas of ancient times as recorded by the Roman builder Vitruvius in his treatise on architecture. On his travels to Rome and southern France, Palladio also made a close study of the Roman buildings that had been preserved, and the results can be seen not only in his own designs, but also in his influential writings. In Italy, more than 60 buildings, churches and city palaces, in addition to villas, were based on his plans. But his influence was also felt in other parts of Europe and, as we have seen when looking at Jefferson's Monticello (see pages 110–111), in the United States.

The Perfect Form

One of his most famous buildings – and certainly the most copied – is the Villa la Rotonda. Originally called the Villa Almerico-Capra, it was built after 1566 outside the city gates of Vicenza. The name by which it is now known comes from the circular

domed hall located exactly in the centre of the villa. The idea of creating a private house as a central-plan building was daring at the time, for this form was generally restricted to sacred buildings. The Rotonda has three floors: the utility rooms were located on the ground floor. The piano nobile, which could be reached by an elegant flight of stairs, was used for entertaining; and the living quarters were located on the mezzanine above. By 1569 the building was almost complete, and its owner, Paolo Almerico, could gaze across the fertile landscape of the region from the luxury of his elegant villa.

From Temple to Villa

Palladio also chose an unusual solution for his decoration of the entrance to the Rotonda by designing it as a temple front: six Ionian columns support a pediment. Palladio describes this design feature in the second of his *Four Books on Architecture*: "In all the villas, and some of the city houses, I have attached the pediment (the temple front) to the façade of the house … in order that these pediments indicate the entrance to the house, and serve also the magnitude and glory of the work in such a way that the front section of the house is elevated above the remaining sections." However, in the Villa la Rotonda, the architect was not satisfied with one temple front: he placed such porticoes on all four sides of the building! By doing without a single main perspective, Palladio stressed the symmetry of the construction: his aim was a classically perfect design in harmony with its setting.

VILLA LA ROTONDA, VICENZA, ITALY
From 1566

Andrea Palladio

1508 Born in Padua, as Andrea di Piero della Gondola
1521 Serves apprenticeship with the stonemason Pietro Cavazza
1524 Settles in Vicenza
1540 Granted the right to call himself an architect
1537 Villa Godi near Vicenza
1542 Palazzo Thiene, Vicenza
1549 Becomes main architect on the renovation of the Palazzo della Ragione, Vicenza
1554 Publishes the guide to the architecture of Rome: *Antichità di Roma*
1565 San Giorgio Maggiore, Venice
ca. 1566 Villa la Rotonda
1570 Published *Four Books on Architecture*
1575 Il Redentore, Venice
1580 Dies 14 August

The entrance to the Villa la Rotonda: an antique temple façade

1556–1605 Height of the Mogul Empire under
Jalaluddin Muhammed Akbar

1588 Sinking of the Spanish Armada

1541 Spain conquers the Mayan kingdom
in Central America

1604 Construction of
the Pont Neuf
in Paris

1500–1550 HIGH RENAISSANCE   LATE RENAISSANCE 1550–1600

1550–1600 LATE RENAISSANCE

| 1520 | 1525 | 1530 | 1535 | 1540 | 1545 | 1550 | 1555 | 1560 | 1565 | 1570 | 1575 | 1580 | 1585 | 1590 | 1595 | 1600 | 1605 |

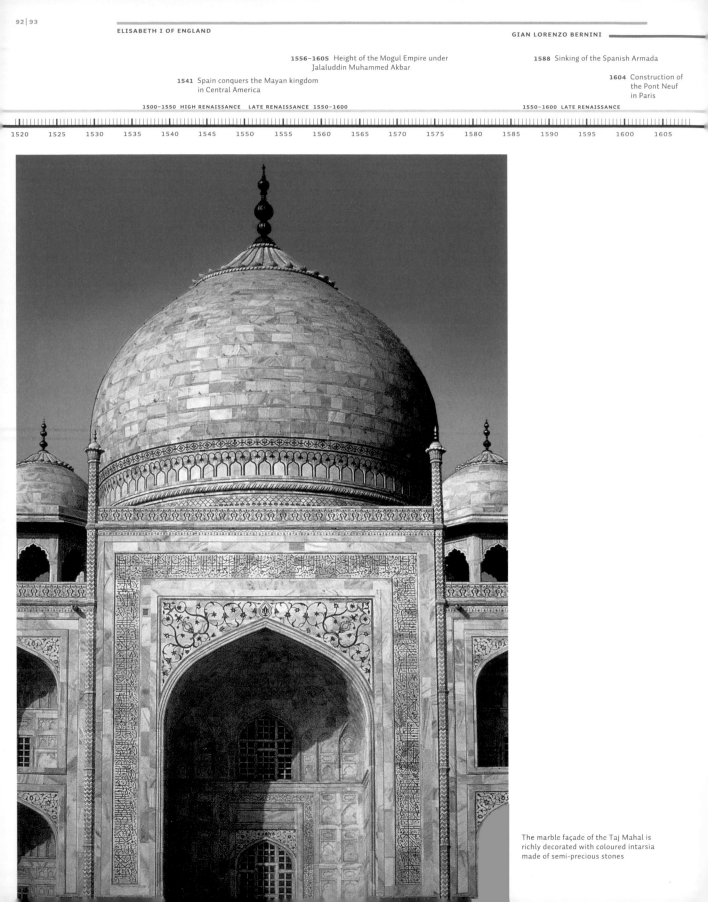

The marble façade of the Taj Mahal is
richly decorated with coloured intarsia
made of semi-precious stones

LOUIS XIV, SUN KING

1614 Founding of New Amsterdam (New York)

1642 *The Company of Frans Banningh Cocq*
(*The Night Watch*), Rembrandt
1643 Louis XIV becomes King of France
1655 Start of British West Indies trade

1600–1730 BAROQUE

1610 1615 1620 1625 1630 1635 1640 1645 1650 1655 1660 1665 1670 1675 1680 1685 1690 1695

TAJ MAHAL

Shah Jahan was inconsolable when his beloved wife Mumtaz Mahal died giving birth to her fourteenth child in 1630. After a two-year mourning period, he threw himself into the construction of a building of previously unknown size and grandeur, bringing together the finest builders and craftsmen in north India to construct and decorate it.

Between 1632 and 1652, around 20,000 people were employed in creating the most famous mausoleum in the world. It stands at the northern edge of a garden in Agra, the capital of the Mogul Empire. Shah Jahan chose dazzling white marble as the building material for his wife's tomb. The entrance, however, is in red sandstone, and so stands in marked contrast to the resplendent white façade. The plan is essentially a square with bevelled edges. The building is crowned with an onion dome, flanked by additional cupolas, turrets and slender minarets. The building is also a masterpiece of technology: the dome itself is 65 metres (213 feet) high and 28 metres (92 feet) wide, rising above a cylindrical lower construction, the drum. This dome cannot be seen in the interior; the burial hall is covered by a hemispherical dome. The construction of the central dome was not the only difficulty the builders had to solve; they also had to adapt the interior to cope with the expected flow of pilgrims. Visitors wanted to walk all around the central burial hall, which connects the four side halls.

Place of Pilgrimage

The shah also had plans for his own final resting place: he intended to build a similar palace, this time of black marble, opposite the Taj Mahal. However, his son, who overthrew him in 1658, to prevent the state's bankruptcy, thwarted these plans: he buried Shah Jahan alongside his beloved wife. Even though there is only one mausoleum, the flood of visitors has not ceased to this very day, and millions have admired the building at first hand. Well, that's how it was until 1996. In that year, the heavy basses of a rock concert shook the Taj Mahal so violently that it was weakened. Since then, the building has not been thrown open to large-scale events and, as a precaution, the 350th anniversary celebrations in 2002 were held two kilometres away. Even the pilgrims who want to see the Taj Mahal by moonlight are subjected to strict rules: on five nights each month, no more than 400 of them are allowed to admire India's most famous building from a viewpoint near the palace. If one believes the words of the 19th-century British artist and poet Edward Lear, it is still worthwhile: "In future, the population of our world will be divided into two classes – those who have seen the Taj Mahal, and those who have not."

TAJ MAHAL, AGRA, INDIA
1632–52

If you want to see the Taj Mahal from your armchair, you can find a comprehensive guide at http://www.taj-mahal.net. There you can enjoy a panoramic overview, from the gatekeeper's lodge to the Garden of Paradise, and from the grave of Mumtaz Mahal to the view from the roof.

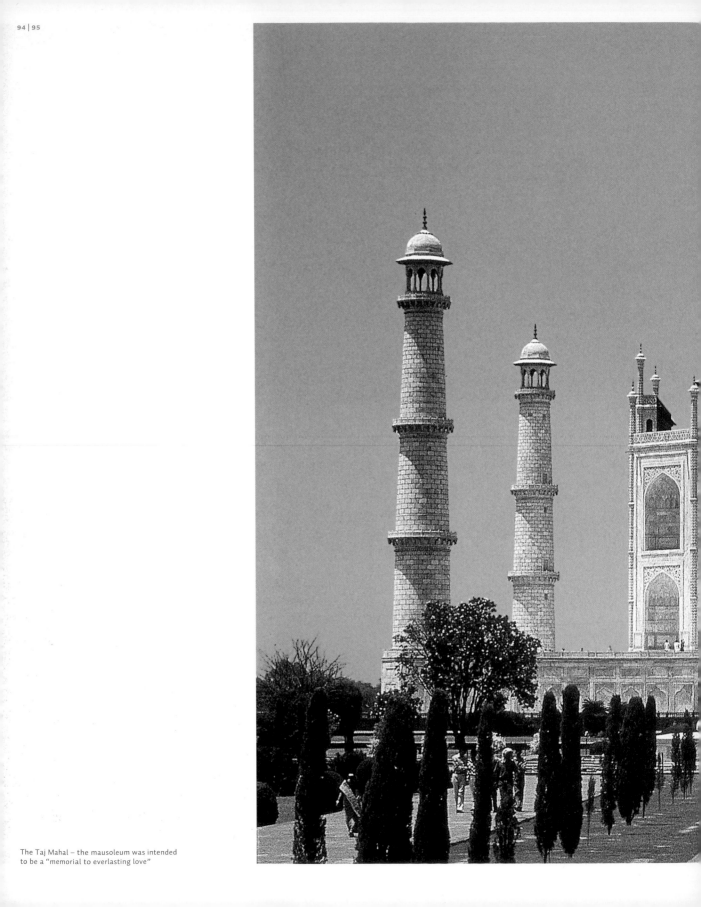

The Taj Mahal – the mausoleum was intended
to be a "memorial to everlasting love"

ca. 1588 Completion of St Peter's dome
following plans by Michelangelo

1618–1648 Thirty Years' War

1602 The Dutch found the Cape Colony in South Africa

1639 English settlement in Madras
(India), later seat of the
East-India Trading Company

1550–1600 LATE RENAISSANCE   BAROQUE 1600–1730

1560   1565   1570   1575   1580   1585   1590   1595   1600   1605   1610   1615   1620   1625   1630   1635   1640   1645

The golden roofs of the palace

below:
The Potala Palace on the Red Mountain

right page:
Staircase in the White Palace

1642 *The Company of Captain Frans Banningh Cocq*
(The Night Watch), Rembrandt

1661 The Jesuits Dorville and Grueber reach
Lhasa, the capital of Tibet

1703 Beginning of construction of
Buckingham Palace in London

1721 Russia becomes a major
European power

1600–1730 BAROQUE

1650   1655   1660   1665   1670   1675   1680   1685   1690   1695   1700   1705   1710   1715   1720   1725   1730   1735

POTALA PALACE

Located just north of the Himalayas, Lhasa, the former capital of Tibet, stands 3,700 metres (9,800 feet)
above sea level. Rising majestically in the centre of the city is the huge Potala Palace complex, one of the few
Tibetan cultural monuments to have survived the Chinese Cultural Revolution.

This palace-monastery completely dominates Lhasa
(which means "place of the gods"). It sits on a
narrow ridge of the Red Mountain, its southern face
being built into the rocks that sweep down to the
Lhasa River. Due to its location and size, the place
complex looks rather like a fortress – it was certainly
necessary to have buildings strong enough to
combat the cold winds on the roof of the world.

The Spiritual Heart of Tibet

The Potala was the seat of the Tibetan government
and official residence of the Dalai Lama, the spiritual
and secular leader of Buddhist Tibet, until 1959. The
Sanskrit word "Potala" means the seat of the
Bodhisattva Avalokiteshvara, and the Dalai Lamas
regarded themselves as the mortal embodiment of
this being, who was striving for spiritual enlightenment. Today, this palace-monastery complex in
Lhasa is a world famous museum. But along with its
most famous temple, the Jokhang Temple, it is still
one of the most important places of pilgrimage for
Tibetan Buddhists.

The Heart of the Complex

The various palaces and temples in the Potala
Palace, which are exemplary for the architecture
of this region, cover an area of 300 x 250 metres
(984 x 820 feet). The major section of the Potala was
constructed during the reign of the fifth Dalai Lama
in the second half of the 17th century. The White
Palace in the north of the complex, which was built
in the short period between 1645 and 1648, forms
its heart. The seven-storey building housed the
administration and was the Dalai Lama's residence.
The largest room of the whitewashed palace, the
Great Eastern Assembly Hall, or Tsomchen Shar,
on the fourth floor, was used for the New Year's
celebrations and the enthronement of the Dalai
Lama. It has a surface area of more than 700 square
metres (7,535 square feet).

Splendour on the Roof of the World

A dazzling red palace with golden roofs and turrets
adjoins on the west, with its numerous temples,
chapels and meditation halls. The Dalai Lama's
private quarters were also located on the highest of
the Red Palace's four storeys. Magnificently decorated *stupas* (Buddhist tombs), where the relics of the
deceased Dalai Lamas were preserved, can also be
found in the Red Palace. The most magnificent tomb
is that of the first builder of the Potala, the fifth
Dalai Lama, in the western temple. His tomb is
decorated with around 3,700 kilos (8,160 pounds) of
gold, as well as precious stones, and rises to a
height of more than 14 metres (50 feet) – almost to
the palace's roof terrace. Stretched out below is the
broad valley of Lhasa.

POTALA PALACE, LHASA, TIBET
Beginning of construction 17th C

The Potala Palace was added to the
UNESCO World Heritage List in 1994.

Today, the building is a museum but
still belongs to the most important
pilgrimage destinations for Tibetan
Buddhists.

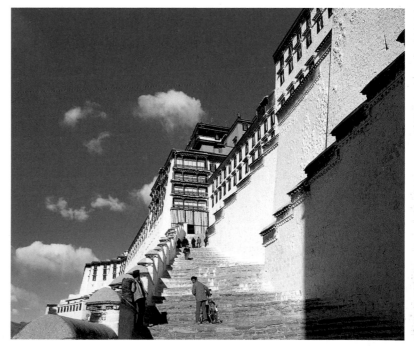

1599–1667 Francesco Borromini,
Late-Baroque architect

1618–1648 Thirty Years' War

1636 Calvinists found Harvard as the first
North American university

1603 New France, first French colony in Canada

1643 Louis XIV becomes King of France

1550–1600 LATE RENAISSANCE   BAROQUE 1600–1730

1580   1585   1590   1595   1600   1605   1610   1615   1620   1625   1630   1635   1640   1645   1650   1655   1660   1665

*View of Versailles Palace and its gardens,
painting by Pierre Patel, 1668*

PETER I, THE GREAT, TSAR OF RUSSIA

1702–1710 Last Huguenot War in France

1672 Beginning of construction of St Paul's Cathedral
in London, Christopher Wren

1720 Beginning of construction of the Würzburg
Residence, Balthasar Neumann

1600–1730 BAROQUE   ROCOCO 1730–1770

| | | | | | | | | | | | | | | | | | |
|1670|1675|1680|1685|1690|1695|1700|1705|1710|1715|1720|1725|1730|1735|1740|1745|1750|1755|

VERSAILLES

When Louis XIV, the Sun King, ascended the throne, France had become a new major European power. Its absolutist royal household needed an appropriate home, and so 30,000 workers and all the major artists in the France worked for decades to create it.

Louis' father had already had a relatively modest hunting lodge constructed in the forest area to the west of Paris. The Roi Soleil, by contrast, thought on a completely different scale. In 1668 he commissioned the architect Louis Le Vau to transform the hunting lodge in Versailles into an impressive palace complex. The façade of the new palace was to stretch over 600 metres (1,970 feet). Ten years later, the architect Jules Hardouin-Mansart took over the supervision of the building work. He had the Gallery of Mirrors, which is 71 metres (233 feet) long, built on the first floor on the garden side; this ornate gallery, completely lined with mirrors, was to be used for court balls and receptions. He also built the south and north wings that surround the main court, which is known as the "court of honour". Fifty years – and an astronomical 500 million gold francs – later, construction was finally completed with the court chapel. For the time being, at least. Louis' successor would add an opera house cum ballroom that could accommodate 700, as well as two pleasure palaces – the Grand and Petit Trianons – in the northern sector of the spacious grounds.

"L'état c'est moi"

Three main avenues lead to the palace, which forms the central point of a gigantic star-shaped layout. The central point of the castle – and, therefore, of the absolutist cosmos – was the royal bedroom and reception room. It was no coincidence that Louis' motto was "L'état c'est moi" (I am the state). In 1682, the king moved to Versailles with his entire court. Approximately 3,000 people lived in the palace, all observing the strict etiquette of the court, and all organized according to their place in the hierarchy. The royal couple lived on the first floor of the central section, the princes and upper aristocracy in the side wings, facing the park; the less privileged courtiers had to make do with less attractive views.

Art and Nature

At the time construction began, the elevation on which the castle was built was surrounded by swampland. Louis had this land drained, but the cost was high: thousands of workers suffered from yellow fever. Over the next decades, a garden landscape, worked out to the last detail, was created on an area of over 800 hectares (3 square miles) under the supervision of André le Nôtre. Small forests were planted, and two canals dug in order to keep the fountains and waterworks supplied. The area was crossed by symmetrical paths flanked by statues and marble urns. The parterre was formed by rigidly geometrical flowerbeds. Straight rows of clipped trees and sculpturally manicured hedges set the scene – nature transformed by art. Both palace and landscape were now fitting settings for elegant receptions and elaborate royal festivities.

VERSAILLES, FRANCE
From 1668

Louis Le Vau

1612 Born in Paris, the son of a builder
1642–44 Hôtel Lambert, Paris
1657 Chateau of Vaux-le-Vicomte
1661/62 Reconstruction of the Galérie d'Apollon in the Louvre
1668 Extensions to the palace of Versailles
1670 Dies in Paris

Jules Hardouin-Mansart

1646 Born in Paris
1675 Royal architect
AFTER 1678, Extension of Palace of Versailles, including the Gallery of Mirrors, the Orangerie and Grand Trianon
1680–91 Les Invalides, Paris
FOLLOWING 1698, Place Vendôme, Paris
1699 Chief court architect
1708 Dies in Marly

André Le Nôtre

1613 Born in Paris
Studies painting, architecture and landscape gardening
1656–61 Park of the Chateau of Vaux-le-Vicomte
1661–90 Versailles Park
1700 Dies in Paris

The Hall of Mirrors

The garden façade of the palace

PETER I, THE GREAT, TSAR OF RUSSIA

BALTHASAR NEUMANN

1648 End of the Thirty Years' War

1668 Beginning of construction of
Versailles Palace

1683 Turks besiege Vienna

| 1615 | 1620 | 1625 | 1630 | 1635 | 1640 | 1645 | 1650 | 1655 | 1660 | 1665 | 1670 | 1675 | 1680 | 1685 | 1690 | 1695 | 1700 |

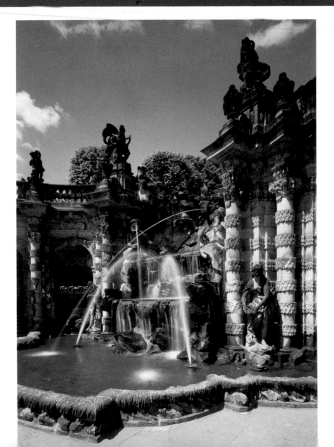

A total work of art from the late-Baroque
period: The Zwinger in Dresden

left:
The Nymphs' Bath with its rich figural
decoration

ZWINGER PALACE

The Zwinger Palace was originally laid out as a garden on the western border of Dresden, but it soon became the historic centre of the city. Fountains in front of curved façades, staircases adorned with sculptures and balustrades — this "total work of art," created in the exuberant spirit of the Baroque, still impresses.

The term "Zwinger" refers to the area or enclosure between two defence walls or ramparts. When Matthäus Daniel Pöppelman began construction in 1709, the idea was not to build a defence fortification for the city, however, but to provide a setting for magnificent courtly festivities.

Wedding Festivities

Speed was of the essence, as the Zwinger was intended to provide the appropriate setting for a very special wedding in 1719. Prince Frederick August, later king, was to marry the Emperor's daughter, Maria Josepha – an event which required a suitably grand venue. However, the Zwinger was not completely finished at the time of the festivities and the side of the building on Theaterplatz, where the picture gallery is located today, was hidden behind a monumental viewing platform. Contemporaries were nevertheless impressed: "Dreaming of paradise would be no less pleasant", was one observation.

Pavilions and galleries are located around the almost square inner courtyard, in which there are four fountains and where two broad pathways

intersect. One leads to the Rampart Pavilion in the north and the Glockenspiel Pavilion in the south. The main entrance is the Crown Gate, a triumphal arch surmounted (appropriately) by a crown-shaped dome.

From Place to Museum

Not all later generations were fond of the late Baroque opulence of the Zwinger. In 1803, the German architect Karl Friedrich Schinkel, who was much more enamoured of the buildings of antiquity, described the Zwinger as "a broad building of ashlars" which was "full of mussels and floral glory in the worst possible style". And indeed Frederick August's taste for elaborate decoration is found everywhere. The main building is covered with stone urns, putti, masks and garlands, and the Nymphs' Bath in the north-eastern section of the complex is particularly rich in sculptural adornment. The nymphs, who give this section its name, stand in the niches of this grotto between cascades, fountains and pools of water. Frederick August commissioned his court sculpture Balthasar Permoser to carve the statues. He himself took care that his collection of art treasures was suitably displayed in the new rooms. The princely collections were a treasure trove of antiques, minerals, scientific instruments and other objects, and can still be admired in the Zwinger today. There's also the armoury, the porcelain collection, and the old-master paintings, for all of which Gottfried Semper erected an extension on the side facing the River Elbe between 1847 and 1855.

Baroque

The Baroque period was the age of political absolutism and, therefore, of the conspicuous display of power, opulence and wealth. The secular and religious worlds were closely linked; the splendour of the churches and monasteries in Europe is in no way different from that of the palaces. The architectural design, all interior décor, and often even the landscape in which the building was set were elements of the Baroque "total work of art". Stretching from around 1600 to the middle of the 18th century, the Baroque style developed throughout Europe, though often with clear national differences. The decorative but much lighter style known as Rococo emerged from late Baroque during the 18th century.

ZWINGER PALACE, DRESDEN, GERMANY
1709–28

Matthäus Daniel Pöppelmann

1662 Born 3 May in Herford, Westphalia
1686 Settles in Dresden
1705 Appointed state builder to August II the Strong
1705–1915 Taschenberg Palace, Dresden
1711/22 Zwinger, Dresden
1736 Dies 17 January in Dresden

Balthasar Perlmoser

1651 Born 13 August in Kammer in Chiemgau, Bavaria
FROM 1677 In the service of the Medici in Florence
FROM 1699 Works as court sculptor in Dresden
FROM 1712 Sculptural work for the Zwinger in Dresden
1732 Dies 20 February in Dresden

BALTHASAR NEUMANN

1648 End of the Thirty Years' War   **1668** Beginning of construction of Versailles   **1699** Austria becomes a
major European power

1665 *The Girl with a Pearl Earring*, Jan Vermeer

1683 Turks besiege Vienna

1625   1630   1635   1640   1645   1650   1655   1660   1665   1670   1675   1680   1685   1690   1695   1700   1705   1710

The representative garden façade of
the palace with the complex of ponds
in front of it

CATHERINE II, THE GREAT,
TSARINA OF RUSSIA

1776 Declaration of Independence in the USA

1740 Frederick II (the Great)
becomes King of Prussia

1789 Start of the
French Revolution

1600–1730 BAROQUE   ROCOCO 1730–1770

1730–1770 ROCOCO   NEO-CLASSICISM 1770–1840

1715   1720   1725   1730   1735   1740   1745   1750   1755   1760   1765   1770   1775   1780   1785   1790   1795   1800

UPPER BELVEDERE

Prince Eugene had worked hard to earn his right to withdraw to his "beautiful view" (belvedere in Italian). The field marshal had been successful in the Turkish Wars and had taken the most important Hungarian fortress in Budapest. It was time to build a monument to himself.

Vienna had successfully warded off the Turkish threat and by 1683 the Ottoman Empire was finally defeated. The city came to life: the population increased, ambitious building projects were undertaken, and "Vienna Gloriosa" flowered. The opulent Baroque style was well suited to the optimism and grandeur of the period. The aristocracy was now finally able to devote itself to fine houses, and the Glacis – an undeveloped area intended to protect the city – was made available as building land. The Austrian general Prince Eugene of Savoy had no intention of missing this opportunity, particularly as his military successes had made him one of the most influential men in the country.

Palace after Palace

Prince Eugene decided to have a garden palace erected on land he owned near the city wall. Between 1714 and 1716, his personal architect, Johann Lukas von Hildebrandt, created the Lower Belvedere – a Baroque summer residence with rooms for daily living and for entertaining, an orangery, and magnificent stables.

However, Eugene's passion for building was not satisfied. Five years later, after the prince had recently retired from military service, Hildebrandt tackled the Upper Belvedere, which lay on a higher section of the terraced garden area. The prince had originally planned a small building that would provide a focal point for his estate. The final result, however, went far beyond the scope of a small garden palace. The building itself consists of several huge pavilions, each of which is of a different height. The corner buildings, with their domed roofs, are particularly prominent. The central section of the palace, with its grand pediment and rich sculptural ornamentation, is particularly impressive – especially when reflected in the artificial lake just in front of the palace.

UPPER BELVEDERE, VIENNA, AUSTRIA
1721–23

Johann Lukas von Hildebrandt

1668 Born 14 November in Genoa, Italy
Studies with Carlo Fontana in Rome
1695/96 Serves as field engineer in Upper Italy
1696 Settles in Vienna
1697 Garden palace Mansfeld-Fondi (today, Palais Schwarzenberg)
1700–13 Works as court engineer in Vienna
1714–16 Lower Belvedere
1723 Becomes court architect
1721–22 Upper Belvedere
1730s Residence in Würzburg
1745 Dies 16 November in Vienna

Palace and Museum

A magnificent staircase leads from the entrance hall on the ground floor to the centre of the building, the Marble Hall, which is richly decorated with stucco and frescoes. No time was wasted in completing the Upper Belvedere, and the lavish interior décor was in place by 1723. The Prince's library and art collection were located on the ground floor of the building. Both palaces are now part of a museum, the Öster-reichische Galerie, with its collections ranging from the Middle Ages to contemporary art. The symmetrical park that links the two places is no less ornate. The fountains, paths and flowerbeds are inhabited by numerous gods hewn in stone. In addition to the leader of the muses, Apollo, the eternal victor Hercules is prominently represented – entirely fitting in a palace built for a military leader.

Prince Eugene's garden at the Belvedere; etching by an unknown artist

The sala terrena on the ground floor

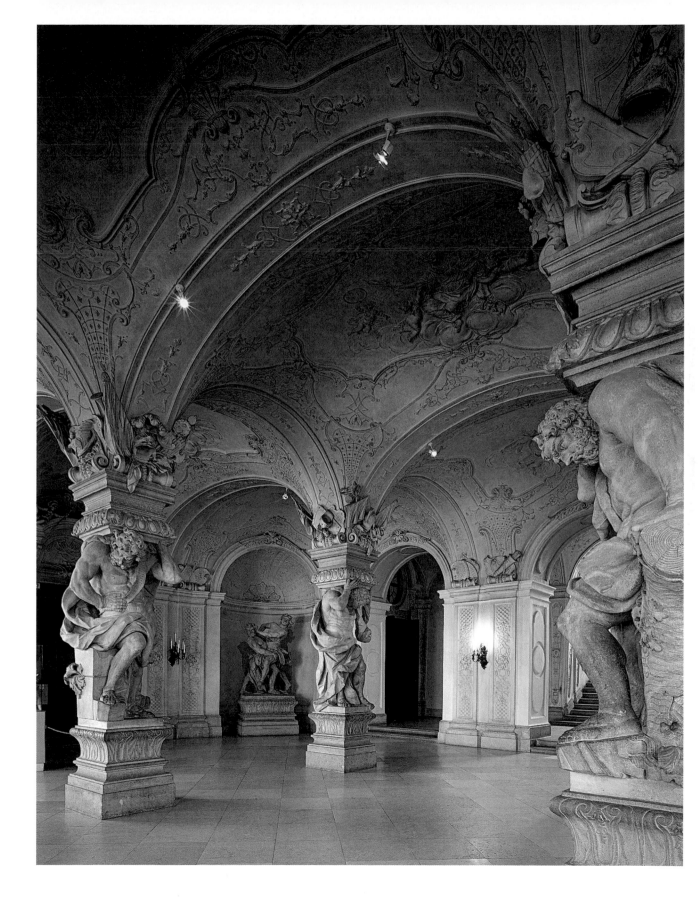

1668 Construction of Versailles Palace

1703 Beginning of construction of
Buckingham Palace in London

1721 Russia becomes a major
European power

1600–1730 BAROQUE   ROCOCO 1730–1770

1650   1655   1660   1665   1670   1675   1680   1685   1690   1695   1700   1705   1710   1715   1720   1725   1730   1735

View from the west over the Jardin des
Tuileries and the Jardins du Carrousel

below:
The glass pyramid in front of the Louvre,
created by the architect Ieoh Ming Pei

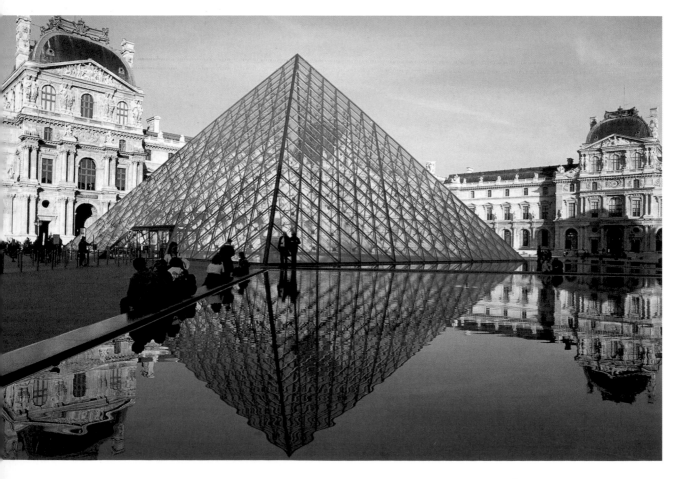

NAPOLEON BONAPARTE

1789 Start of the French Revolution

1776 Declaration of Independence in the USA

1792 France becomes a republic

1804 Napoleon Bonaparte
becomes French Emperor

1791 Construction of the Brandenburg Gate in Berlin

1730–1770 ROCOCO   NEO-CLASSICISM 1770–1840

1740   1745   1750   1755   1760   1765   1770   1775   1780   1785   1790   1795   1800   1805   1810   1815   1820   1825

THE LOUVRE

Countless builders were occupied for centuries on this building complex in the heart of Paris. The Louvre was transformed from a castle into a palace, and then from a royal residence into one of the largest museums in the world.

At the end of the 12th century, King Philippe II had Paris – at the time, the largest city in Europe – fortified: a rectangular castle with a solitary round tower was erected on the right bank of the Seine. Philippe's successors had other ideas, however, and the castle was merely to be the modest foundation for what today is the Louvre.

From Castle to Palace

Francis I was a great admirer of Italian Renaissance architecture and in 1546 commissioned the court architect Pierre Lescot to carry out large-scale renovations based on Italian models. The result was more like a new building than a renovation, for the King had the entire west section of the castle demolished and rebuilt. The intention was to convert the medieval castle into a modern palace. A four-sided court, flanked by two-storey buildings, was planned, but Lescot was able to complete only the west and southern sections, which were richly decorated with sculptures by the leading sculptor Jean Goujon. The windows of the two floors are framed with pediments, and the magnificent door-ways are reminiscent of ancient triumphal arches.

In the 17th century, work commenced on the east wing. The celebrated sculptor and architect Gian-lorenzo Bernini, a leading representative of Italian Baroque, submitted plans, but the commission was finally granted to the French architect Perrault, who designed a magnificent colonnade. However, Louis XVI was now becoming more and more interested in another project, the extension of the palace at Versailles (see pages 98–101). The Louvre had out-lived its usefulness as a royal residence. Junk dealers settled in the courtyard, the royal academies took over many of the rooms that had already been completed, and artists used the remaining rooms as studios. It was not until the middle of the 18th century that the courtside façade of the Cour Carré was completed. After this, a lack of funds prevented further building. It had had taken on its present appearance by the middle of the 18th century.

From Palace to Museum

The fate of the Louvre was sealed in 1793, the year of the French Revolution. The doors of the former royal palace were thrown open as the first public art museum. Five years later, the Musée d'Architecture was installed in its elegant rooms. However, artists still determined life in the Louvre; it was difficult to rid itself of its role as a gigantic studio. In order to create space for the artworks that Napoleon had seized as he invaded one European country after another, the architects Percier and Fontaine began the construction of the north wing.

In 1981, under President Mitterand, the decision was taken to use all of the rooms as a museum. The Louvre was once again turned into an enormous building site. This time, the American-Chinese architect Ieoh Ming Pei was in charge, and since 1989 his glass pyramid in the centre of the Cour Napoléon has formed the striking entrance to the Louvre.

THE LOUVRE, PARIS, FRANCE
Beginning of construction 12th century

FACT FILE
Main building period 1546 to mid 18th C
Use Museum, since 1793
Exhibition space 60,000 sq m/
    645,830 sq ft
Number of artworks Approx. 35,000
Departments Oriental Antiquities;
    Egyptian Antiquities; Greek,
    Etruscan and Roman Antiquities;
    Islamic Art; Sculptures; Objets
    d'art; Paintings; Prints and
    Drawings
Visitors Approx. 6 million annually

The Louvre gives information on its building history, as well as recent acquisitions, at http://www.louvre.fr/llv/commun/home_flash.jsp?bmLocale=en. This site allows you to make a virtual visit both to the collections and also to the adjacent Tuileries Gardens.

The Louvre in the *Book of Hours of the Duc de Berry* 1413-16

1703 Beginning of construction of
Buckingham Palace in London

1748 *Portrait of Mr and Mrs Andrews,*
Thomas Gainsborough

1600–1730 BAROQUE   ROCOCO 1730–1770

| 1680 | 1685 | 1690 | 1695 | 1700 | 1705 | 1710 | 1715 | 1720 | 1725 | 1730 | 1735 | 1740 | 1745 | 1750 | 1755 | 1760 | 1765 |

The President's country
house: Monticello near
Charlottesville

right:
Thomas Jefferson's sketch
of the façade of Monticello

Neo-Classicism

Renaissance architects had made an understanding of ancient Roman buildings an essential part of architectural study. In the 1760s, the French revolutionaries rediscovered ancient Greece and Rome and regarded their democratic and republican ideals as an inspiration. And not just in politics: a revival of ancient Greek and Roman building styles was another result. France was not alone: Neo-Classical styles flourished in Germany, Britain, the United States and elsewhere, often taking on its own regional or national character. In the 19th century, architects in Europe and North America added other architectural traditions styles to their repertoire, ranging from medieval Gothic to traditional Chinese.

NAPOLEON BONAPARTE

1789 Start of the French Revolution

1776 Declaration of Independence in the USA

1804 Napoleon Bonaparte
becomes French Emperor

1826 First photograph

1792 France becomes a republic

NEO-CLASSICISM 1770–1840

1770–1840 NEO-CLASSICISM REVIVALISM 1840–1895

| 1770 | 1775 | 1780 | 1785 | 1790 | 1795 | 1800 | 1805 | 1810 | 1815 | 1820 | 1825 | 1830 | 1835 | 1840 | 1845 | 1850 | 1855 |

MONTICELLO

Thomas Jefferson gave his property just outside the small town of Charlottesville the mellifluous name of Monticello. Begun around 1770, this country house, following the formal language of Italian models, was built on the "small mountain" in the midst of an old tobacco plantation.

The governor of Virginia, foreign minister and later the third president of the United States, Jefferson was a man of many talents. He was interested in the natural sciences and philosophy, and was an amateur archaeologist. And despite his work as a lawyer and politician, he still found time to devote himself to building. In addition to public buildings, including the University of Virginia, Jefferson took on the planning of his own country seat. History played a key role in his designs: the United States was still a young Republic, and its culture, politics and architecture drew upon principles of ancient Republican Rome. The epitome of ancient Roman architecture was the Pantheon, a temple consecrated to all the Gods.

Perfect Harmony

The main entrance seems better suited to a Roman temple than a country house: sturdy columns support a profiled cornice on which rests a pediment. Two side wings on the left and right recede from the prominent portico. The white columns and window frames contrast effectively with the red of the bricks. The central dome, rising behind the portico, is also white. Harmony was the guiding principle, and the entire complex is exactly symmetrical. Columned vestibules on both the front and back of the house lead into the interior, and everywhere horizontal and vertical elements complement each other in perfect harmony.

Renaissance Inspiration

Thomas Jefferson was not the first person to value ancient buildings as a source of inspiration. Renaissance architects in particular had studied them closely. One of these was the Italian architect Andrea Palladio, who in the 16th century built numerous country villas in the Veneto region close to Venice. It was his designs in particular that served as models in the 18th century. His Villa Rotonda, a central-plan building near Vicenza, is one of his most ingenious and influential designs (see pages 90–91). Jefferson was greatly attracted to Palladio's restrained classicism when designing Montecello. He withdrew to this country seat when he retired from politics, though it was not to enjoy a quiet life. He had many cultural and scientific interests, as shown by his library, which contained more than 6,000 volumes on all manner of subject. These would later form the basis for the collection of the Library of Congress in Washington, D.C.

MONTICELLO, CHARLOTTESVILLE, USA
ca. 1770

Thomas Jefferson

1743 Born 13 April in Albemarle County, Virginia
1760s Studies law
FROM 1767 Works as an attorney
1772 Marries Martha Wayles Skelton
1774 Becomes Representative for Virginia in Congress. Works on the colonies' Declaration of Independence
1779–81 Governor of Virginia
1785–89 Serves as diplomat in France; after his return to the USA, becomes Foreign Minister
1785–92 Virginia State Capitol built to his design
1796 Becomes Vice President
1801–09 Serves as third President of the USA
1826 Dies 4 July in Monticello, Virginia

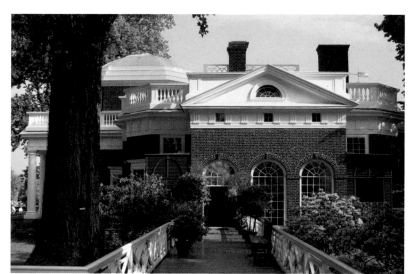

The back of the property

1703 Beginning of construction of
Buckingham Palace in London

1600–1730 BAROQUE   ROCOCO 1730–1770

| 1680 | 1685 | 1690 | 1695 | 1700 | 1705 | 1710 | 1715 | 1720 | 1725 | 1730 | 1735 | 1740 | 1745 | 1750 | 1755 | 1760 | 1765 |

Royal Crescent – a semi-circular
row of houses

NAPOLEON BONAPARTE

1789 Start of the French Revolution

1793 *The Death of Marat*, Jacques-Louis David

1804 Napoleon Bonaparte becomes French Emperor

1815 Napoleon overwhelmingly defeated at Waterloo

1826 First photograph

NEO-CLASSICISM 1770–1840

1770–1840 NEO-CLASSICISM   REVIVALISM 1840–1895

1770   1775   1780   1785   1790   1795   1800   1805   1810   1815   1820   1825   1830   1835   1840   1845   1850   1855

ROYAL CRESCENT

Bath, a small town in the west of England, developed into a fashionable spa in the 18th century. The city planners faced the task of trying to create an attractive and well-organised urban environment that met all the needs of their wealthy guests.

The writer Johanna Schopenhauer, the mother of the celebrated German philosopher Arthur Schopenhauer, stayed in Bath during her trip to England in 1787, and reported that "the entire city is an enormous hôtel garni". Hotels, theatres, ball rooms and coffee houses were erected as social meeting places, promenades created for the essential "stroll through the town", and the roads carrying visitor and goods around the town were greatly improved. Above all, more housing was needed: the population of what had become the most important British spa increased tenfold during the 18th century.

Father and Son

John Wood the Younger, following in his father's footsteps as an architect, played an important role in creating the city's new appearance. John Wood the Elder had planned Queen Square, followed around the middle of the century by The Circus, with its circular plan. In 1767, his son started work on the row of houses to be called the Royal Crescent, located not far from The Circus. The name comes from the shape of the row, which resembles that of a crescent moon. This semi-circular row of large urban villas lies on a slope in the large Royal Victoria Park. The open side of the crescent faces a broad lawn and provides a fine view of the city. Here the architect had turned his back on the contemporary ideals of urban construction, which favoured closed forms.

Classical Inspiration

The fronts of the 30 houses of the Royal Crescent (which in effect create a singe façade) are decorated in exactly the same way. The ground floor, above the basement, which was originally planned for the staff, is not subdivided. The upper storeys, by contrast, have tall Ionian columns between the windows. These half-columns stretch over two storeys, in a style known as the "giant order". The absence of any further accentuation of individual building components is typical of the Georgian era, when the building boom in Bath took place. The symmetrical structure of the façade and floor plan is typical for this restrained style, as is a return to the architecture of classical antiquity, which can be seen above all in the columns and arches. Though there is now a hotel in the centre of the Royal Crescent, most of the houses are still family homes, and still enjoy a fine view of the city.

ROYAL CRESCENT, BATH, ENGLAND
1767–74

John Wood the Younger

1728 Born 25 February in Bath
1754–64 Continues with The Circus, begun by his father
1767–74 Builds Royal Crescent
1769–71 Builds Assembly Halls in Bath (today the Costume Museum)
1781 Dies 18 June in Bath

The house at number 1 Royal Crescent is now a museum and gives a vivid impression of the interior decoration of the houses on crescent in the 18th century: http://bath-preservation-trust.org.uk/index.php?id=3.

Ionic columns unite the two upper stories

NAPOLEON BONAPARTE

1721 Russia becomes a major European power

1760 England conquers Canada

1776 Declaration of Independence in the USA

1789 George Washington becomes first President of the USA

1600–1730 BAROQUE ROCOCO 1730–1770

1730–1770 ROCOCO NEO-CLASSICISM 1770–1840

| 1705 | 1710 | 1715 | 1720 | 1725 | 1730 | 1735 | 1740 | 1745 | 1750 | 1755 | 1760 | 1765 | 1770 | 1775 | 1780 | 1785 | 1790 |

The illuminated Capitol

1791 Construction of the Brandenburg Gate in Berlin

1848 *The Communist Manifesto,* Marx/Engels

1804 Napoleon Bonaparte becomes French Emperor

1863 *Déjeuner sur l'Herbe,* Édouard Manet

1770–1840 NEO-CLASSICISM REVIVALISM 1840–1895

| 1795 | 1800 | 1805 | 1810 | 1815 | 1820 | 1825 | 1830 | 1835 | 1840 | 1845 | 1850 | 1855 | 1860 | 1865 | 1870 | 1875 | 1880 |

UNITED STATES CAPITOL

The dazzling white Capitol stands proudly at the eastern end of Washington's National Mall. It was planned as the seat of government of the – then very young – United States, yet its builders looked back to the Europe of ancient times for inspiration.

In 1776, the 13 foundation states of the United States declared themselves independent of Britain. This led to a great increase in the number of new buildings, particularly those for the new government institutions. The parliament building was to be the chief expression of the social and political ideals of the country. Ancient Greece and Rome provided both the political and architectural inspiration, with the Capitol becoming one of the finest examples of American Neo-Classicism.

In Rome's Footsteps

It was intended that the representatives of the American people should meet on Capitol Hill, named after the most important of the Seven Hills of Rome. The parliament was named the Senate – an additional indication of the influence of ancient Rome. In 1793, George Washington finally laid the cornerstone for the Capitol: the city of Washington was later built around it.

The young architect William Thornton was responsible for the plans. However, the list of architects and builders became longer and longer as various renovations and extensions were undertaken over the following decades. The building soon proved to be too small to accommodate the representatives of all the states. It was originally planned for the 13 founding states, but the number had more than doubled since the beginning of construction. The size of the Capitol was doubled accordingly: two additional parts were created for the Senate and House of Representatives.

The circular central building is approximately 60 metres (200 feet) high, with columned vestibules to the east and west. North and south wings were added later. A flag indicates which house is in session. Thomas Walter crowned the building with the huge dome in 1865. To this day, it has remained the emblem not only of the capitol city but also of the American belief in progress: Walter used 4,000 tons of cast iron – a completely new building material at the time – for the two shells forming the dome.

UNITED STATES CAPITOL,
WASHINGTON, D.C., USA
From 1793

CHRONOLOGY
1793 Foundation stone laid by George Washington
1801 The Supreme Court meets in the Capitol for the first time
1803 Benjamin Henry Latrobe commissioned by President Jefferson to continue construction
1810 The Senate moves into the north wing
1814 British troops burn the Capitol to the ground
1815–17 Latrobe began the reconstruction
1818 Charles Bulfinch becomes Latrobe's successor
1819 Supreme Court, Senate and House of Representatives meet in the Capitol
1850 Competition for extensions to the Capitol held
1851 Foundation stone laid for the extensions planned by the architect Thomas U. Walter
1865 Walter completes the dome
1935 The Supreme Court receives its own building

The homepage at:
http://www.aoc.gov/cc/index.cfm gives an impression of the size and layout of the building complex. The Capitol's Visitors' Center, with information on the present restoration work, is also available online.

A woodcut of The New Senate in the Capitol from 1859

The Capitol is the geographical central
point of Washington; its cupola is still
the city's emblem

A Quick Tour

The Capitol is not merely a building: it's a city within a city. Every working day, around 20,000 people make their way between the Dome and the six Legislative Buildings, and it's not difficult to get lost in the 850 corridors. The many millions of visitors who come to Capitol Hill every year are drawn there not only by the offices and assembly halls, but also by an impressive art collection. The Capitol is guarded by its own police, who keep a close eye on the large number of demonstrators who want to draw attention to their causes in front of this symbol of America's political life and national identity.

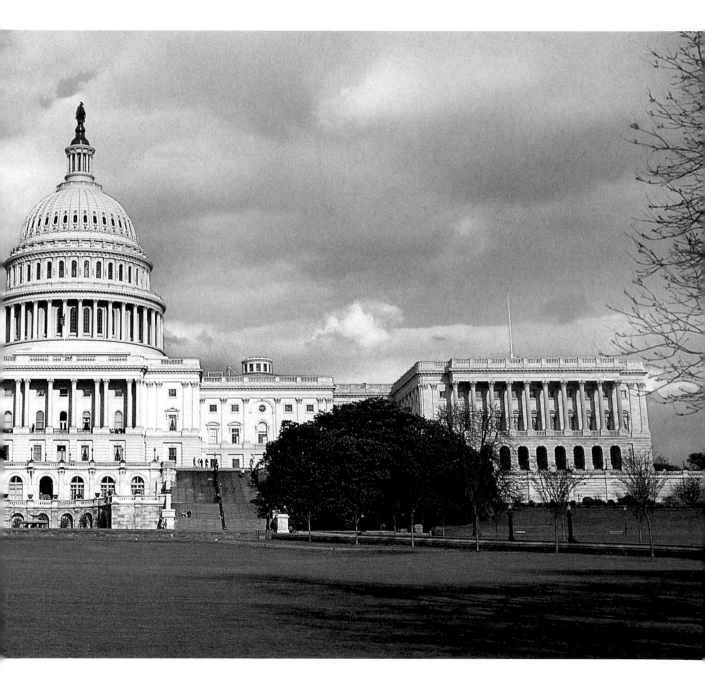

1844 *Rain, Steam and Speed*, JMW Turner

1826 First photograph

1848 *The Communist Manifesto*, Marx/Engels

1871 Wilhelm I becomes German Emperor

1770–1840 NEO-CLASSICISM   REVIVALISM 1840–1895

| 1795 | 1800 | 1805 | 1810 | 1815 | 1820 | 1825 | 1830 | 1835 | 1840 | 1845 | 1850 | 1855 | 1860 | 1865 | 1870 | 1875 | 1880 |

La Sagrada Família – still unfinished today

ERICH MENDELSOHN, ARCHITECT

1887–1889 Construction of the
Eiffel Tower in Paris

1914–1918 First World War

1931 Empire State Building, New York,
the highest building in the world

1921 Albert Einstein, Nobel Prize
for his quantum theory

1840–1895 REVIVALISM   1895–1910 ART NOUVEAU   MODERNISM 1910–1980

1885   1890   1895   1900   1905   1910   1915   1920   1925   1930   1935   1940   1945   1950   1955   1960   1965   1970

LA SAGRADA FAMÍLIA

One of the world's most famous buildings, the church of La Sagrada Família (Catalan for Holy Family) is situated in the centre of the Spanish city of Barcelona. The architect Antoní Gaudí y Cornet devoted three decades of his life to the building of the church, and it may not be completed until 2050.

The beginning of his career was not very promising: the Catalan Gaudí graduated from university with the lowest grade possible, a mere "passed". However, he soon found an influential client in the entrepreneur Eusebi Güell, and made a name for himself with numerous buildings in Barcelona. In 1883, when Gaudí started working on the Sagrada Família (he was only 33 years old), the crypt was already under construction. The neo-Gothic plans for the church had been drawn up by the architect del Villar, who had started construction one year before. Gaudí continued with Gothic forms, but not for long. His inspiration was not the architecture of the Middle Ages, but nature: the pillars and supports look like trees, with their branches and stone leaves, and there are flowers, insects and other creatures everywhere. Gaudí decided on round forms and extravagant, knob-like capitals for the planned 12 bell-towers – one for each of the Apostles. Colour symbolism was also given its due: the Door of Hope on the west was planned to glow in hues of green.

A Sermon in Stone

The basic shape of the Sagrada Família is a cross, but the circle is almost more important. According to Gaudí: "The straight line is the line of mankind; the curve is the line of God." His notion of a "sermon in stone" may explain why he devoted so much space for the sung praise of God: there's room for 1,500 singers in the galleries and five organs.

Potentially, at least. When the architect died in a road accident in 1926, most of the information on the Sagrada Família was in the form of plans and a plaster model. Only one of three façades – on the east – was under construction, and the east portal, with its depiction of the Nativity, was not yet completed. Even today, the towers – the highest is planned to soar 170 metres (558 feet) into the sky – still stand side by side with construction cranes. This is not just because of Gaudí's complicated plans, which are full of detail and rich in symbolism. The

Sagrada Família was planned as a "penance church", to be built exclusively from voluntary contributions. Particularly during the First World War, the financial resources available for the building work were meagre, and Gaudí himself had to help find people willing to make donations. The church has consumed incredible sums and even now is making only slow progress. Gaudí would probably bear it with fortitude: he understood that "God is not in a hurry".

Art Nouveau

Around 1900, when science and technology were developing rapidly, many architects, sculptors and painters, as well as carpenters, glaziers and jewellers, looked back to the traditional craftsmanship of past centuries. They were passionate about sweeping lines and decorative ornaments. The movement had different names in different countries: Jugendstil, Art Nouveau or Modernism. The appearance of Barcelona was transformed by Antoní Gaudí, Lluis Domènech i Montaner, and others. They integrated a great variety of stylistic quotations into their residential buildings, parks and public buildings, and used mosaics, glazed ceramics and other craft techniques to created colourful, asymmetrical designs strongly influenced by nature, and in particular by plant forms.

LA SAGRADA FAMÍLIA, BARCELONA, SPAIN
Beginning of construction 1882

Antoni Gaudí y Cornet

1852 Born in Reus, Catalonia, Spain
1878 Completes architecture studies in Barcelona
1883–85 Villa Quijano (El Capricho) in Comillas, Cantabria; Casa Vicens, Barcelona
1883–1926 La Sagrada Família, Barcelona
1886–90 Palacio Güell, Barcelona
1887–93 Archbishop's Palace in Astorga, León
1889–90 Colegio de las Teresianas, Barcelona
1900–14 Park Güell, Barcelona
1904–06 Casa Batlló, Barcelona
1906–10 Casa Milà (La Pedrera), Barcelona
1926 Dies in Barcelona

The homepage
http://www.sagradafamilia.org/
gives information on progress on the construction of the Sagrada Família.

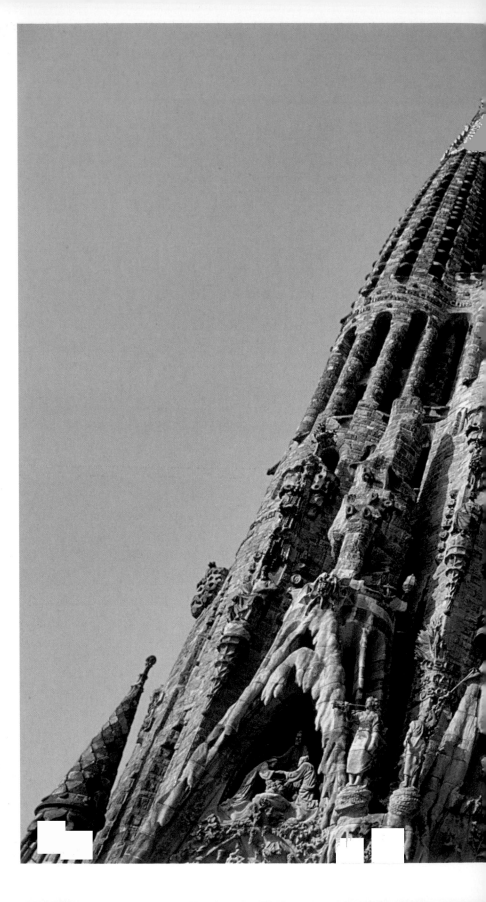

Floor plan and view of the façade towers

1830 Liverpool-Manchester railway

1852 Charles Louis Napoleon
becomes Napoleon III

1876 Invention of
the telephone

1871 Wilhelm I becomes
German Emperor

1770–1840 NEO-CLASSICISM   REVIVALISM 1840–1895

1795   1800   1805   1810   1815   1820   1825   1830   1835   1840   1845   1850   1855   1860   1865   1870   1875   1880

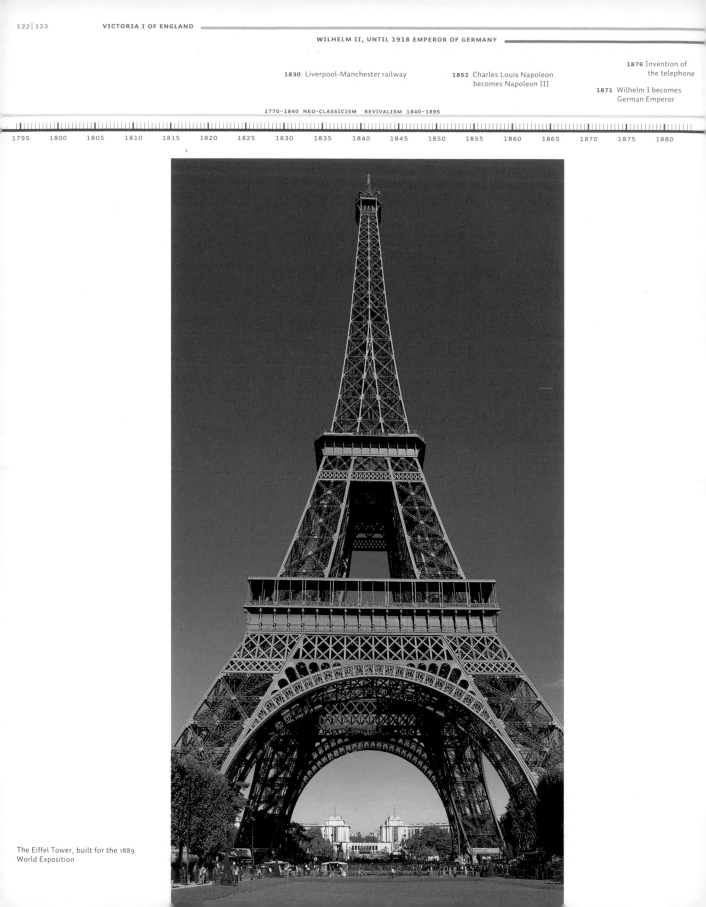

The Eiffel Tower, built for the 1889
World Exposition

ERICH MENDELSOHN, ARCHITECT

1910 Futurist Manifesto, Italy

1931 Empire State Building, New York,
the highest building in the world

1897–1899 Water Lily Pond, Claude Monet   1914–1918 First World War

1840–1895 REVIVALISM   1895–1910 ART NOUVEAU   MODERNISM 1910–1980

1885   1890   1895   1900   1905   1910   1915   1920   1925   1930   1935   1940   1945   1950   1955   1960   1965   1970

THE EIFFEL TOWER

In 1889, no one expected that this temporary metal tower would become the symbol of Paris, and indeed France. Quite the contrary: the Eiffel Tower, which had been constructed for the Paris World Exposition, was widely ridiculed. The writer Guy de Maupassant considered the tower a "skinny pyramid of iron ladders" — and that was almost a compliment.

Though almost 300 metres (984 feet) high, this metal construction – for many years the tallest building in the world – was erected in a mere two years. The tower was made of 12,000 individual parts held together by 2.5 million rivets. Eiffel and his colleagues required 5,300 drawings to plan the construction. Their design and their construction techniques guaranteed maximum stability with minimum weight. But not everybody was convinced. One man living on the Champs de Mars nearby went to court out of fear that the tower could collapse on his house. That was not the only concern troubling Eiffel's contemporaries. Critics initially called the building a "tragic lamp-post" and talked about "a disgusting column of riveted metal".

Its Many Uses
The use of iron as a construction material was, in itself, novel. And not hiding this framework behind stone or brick was revolutionary. Four columns rise up from a square base and finally come together to form a peak at a dizzy height. A network of struts fill the area in between the columns to give the structure great strength and stability. The four large arches at the base were added later because the critics thought that the tower looked bare.

Another criticism was that this metal tower, which was originally meant to be a temporary structure,
had no real function. Well, at least science found a use for it, when an observatory and laboratory for the collection meteorological data were added. And above all it became a major tourist attraction. A platform with restaurants and sales booths was located 57 metres (187 feet) above the ground, and there was an additional opportunity for seeing Paris from above at a height of 115 metres (377 feet). Its eight lifts transported 4,200 visitors – those who found the 1,710 stairs two wearisome – every day. And, in 1921, the antenna on the Eiffel Tower transmitted Europe's first public radio broadcast.

Upward Investment
The entrepreneur Eiffel bore the lion's share of the costs of 6.5 million francs himself and so had the right to use the tower for 20 years. The two million paying visitors during the World Exposition soon made it clear that it would be a worthwhile investment for Eiffel, who had already started to make a profit by 1890. And he was proven right with his reasons for his plan: "The tower can be seen as worthy of representing the art of the modern engineer and the century of industry and science, whose foundations were laid during the Revolution of 1789."

THE EIFFEL TOWER, PARIS, FRANCE
1887–89

Gustave Eiffel

1832 Born in Dijon
1867 Maison Eiffel
1876 Engineer on the construction of the Bon Marché department store, Paris
1877 Bridge over the Douro
1880–84 Garabit Bridge
1885 Participates in the building of the Statue of Liberty in New York
1889 Eiffel Tower
1923 Dies in Paris

The Eiffel Tower was erected in a mere two years by 300 workers

1834 First practicable electric motor

1871 Wilhelm I becomes
German Emperor

1770–1840 NEO-CLASSICISM   REVIVALISM 1840–1895

1795 1800 1805 1810 1815 1820 1825 1830 1835 1840 1845 1850 1855 1860 1865 1870 1875 1880

ERICH MENDELSOHN, ARCHITECT

1886 Statue of Liberty, New York

1891 End of the Indian Wars in the USA

1907 *Les Demoiselles d'Avignon*, Picasso

1910 Futurist Manifesto, Italy

1914–1918 First World War

1931 Empire State Building, New York, the highest building in the world

1840–1895 REVIVALISM   1895–1910 ART NOUVEAU   MODERNISM 1910–1980

1885 1890 1895 1900 1905 1910 1915 1920 1925 1930 1935 1940 1945 1950 1955 1960 1965 1970

CARSON PIRIE SCOTT BUILDING

Chicago, the birthplace of the skyscraper, can boast a great many exceptional examples of modern architecture. Among the architects who changed the face of the city in the last quarter of the 19th century, by far the most influential was Louis Henry Sullivan.

It was Sullivan's conviction that a building should show what went on inside it: its function, whether warehouse, office or home. There was nothing wrong with decoration, insisted Sullivan, as long as it harmonized with the function: structure, function and appearance should be in complete harmony. He had a very clear conception of the skyscraper, which was still in its infancy: "It has to be high, every inch of it has to be high. The strength and force of the height must be integral to it – the magnificence and pride of enthusiasm."

Chicago Shoots Up

Chicago was the ideal city for the Boston-born architect. After the Great Fire of 1871, it was necessary to erect many new buildings in a short time, and they had to be modern and inexpensive. And in order to keep to the existing plan of the city, development had to be upwards: there was little room to spread outwards. Chicago's first steel-framed building – the Home Insurance Building – was erected in the 1880. As the steel frame carried the main weight of a building, there was no longer any need for thick walls, and so architects now had greater liberty to decorate the façades. This building technique also made it possible to greatly increase the number of windows, a fact important in the development of the department stores, which were then just beginning. In the following years, additional commercial and office buildings made of metal and glass shot up. Between 1899 and 1904, Sullivan created one of the most important buildings of the Chicago School – the Schlesinger & Mayer Store, known today as the Carson Pirie Scott Building, which was built as a department store.

Glass and Steel

The rich ornamentation of the two lower floors of the building contrasts greatly with the simplicity of those above. In these upper floors, both the horizontal and vertical lines are strongly emphasised,

creating a cell-like appearance (all the more pronounced because the windows are deeply recessed). These lines in effect reveal rather than conceal the underlying structure of the building, a fact that reflects a new honest in designs. The bold, almost brutal, linearity of the façades is softened by the main corner, which is round. It is at the bottom of this tower-like feature than the main entrance to the department store is located. Unlike most of the building, this entrance is elaborately decorated with wrought iron, and so is a clear focal point at ground level. The entrance and elaborate display windows are meant to encourage passers-by to gaze into, and then enter, this temple of commerce.

Skyscrapers

Initially, skyscrapers were built mainly in Chicago in the aftermath of the Great Fire of 1871, and at first they were called "cloud scrapers". What made their unheard-of height possible was the use of steel frames; walls no longer had to support the building, and so they could be covered in huge areas of glass. Buildings were now so tall, lifts had to be used rather than stairways. The basic design changed little over the years.

The fashion for the skyscraper soon made its way from Chicago to New York, which was soon completely transformed by them. Originally, they were office buildings, but by the 1930s they were also being built as apartment blocks. The development of skyscrapers was encouraged by a desire to erect the world's highest building, a title long help by the Empire State Building in New York. At the moment, the Taiwan International Financial Center, better known as Taipei 101 on account of the number of floors, is the world's highest building, reaching an astonishing height of 508 metres (1,650 feet).

CARSON PIRIE SCOTT BUILDING, CHICAGO, USA
1899–1904

Louis Henry Sullivan

1856 Born in Boston
Studies at the Massachusetts Institute of Technology
1873 Moves to Chicago
1874/75 Studies in Paris
1881 Becomes partner of the architect and engineer Dankmar Adler
1886–89 Auditorium Building, Chicago, in collaboration with Adler
1890/91 Wainwright Building, St Louis
1894–96 Guarantee Building, Buffalo, in collaboration with Adler
1899–1904 Schlesinger & Mayer Store, Chicago (today Carson Pirie Scott Building)
1924 Dies in Chicago

The Carson Pirie Scott Department Store – lavish ornamentation of the two lower storeys

LUDWIG MIES VAN DER ROHE, ARCHITECT

ADOLF HITLER

1871 Wilhelm I becomes Emperor of Germany

1883 First petrol-driven automobile,
Gottlieb Daimler and Carl Benz

1905/1907 Foundation of
Die Brücke and *Der Blaue
Reiter* art groups

1770–1840 NEO-CLASSICISM   REVIVALISM 1840–1895

1840–1895 REVIVALISM   1895–1910 ART NOUVEAU

| 1830 | 1835 | 1840 | 1845 | 1850 | 1855 | 1860 | 1865 | 1870 | 1875 | 1880 | 1885 | 1890 | 1895 | 1900 | 1905 | 1910 | 1915 |

above:
The Bauhaus in Dessau, strictly
functional

below:
Bauhaus – the name of the art
school soon developed into a
stylistic expression

1933 Adolf Hitler becomes Führer
and Chancellor of the Reich

1952 Elvis Presley becomes popular

1914–1918 First World War

1939–1945 Second World War

1961 Berlin Wall erected

MODERNISM 1910–1980

1910–1980 MODERNISM   POST-MODERNISM FROM 1980

1920 1925 1930 1935 1940 1945 1950 1955 1960 1965 1970 1975 1980 1985 1990 1995 2000 2005

BAUHAUS

The German architect and designer Walter Gropius brought a breath of fresh air to the School of Applied Arts in Weimar in 1919. "Bauhaus" was the new name for the arts school where artists, craftsmen and, later, architects worked hand in hand. "Bauhaus" was soon to be the name of the style created by Gropius and his colleagues.

Cubic building elements, clear white surfaces and symmetric rows of windows – Gropius' buildings appear to be severe and entirely functional. His approach dominated the curriculum of the school and caused a worldwide sensation as the "International Style". It was above all through his design for the Bauhaus building that his influence spread. So it's hard to believe that this sought-after architect was a not natural draftsman: as a student, he wrote to his mother that he was "not capable of drawing a straight line".

Good Design at Affordable Prices

This had no effect on his later designs, however (he always had assistants for drawing up plans!). His designs, which included both industrial and residential projects, were based on the belief that well-designed buildings could be made inexpensively through the use of standardised, prefabricated elements to be assembled, literally, like building blocks – good quality mass production for the masses. His plans included satellite towns and residential high-rise buildings, ideas violently criticized at the time. His guiding principle was that "artistic design is not a luxury but must always be a part of life itself". He brought these ideas into the designing of the Bauhaus building, which is one of the best examples of his architecture. It had to be built when the Bauhaus School moved to Dessau in 1925. It's an elegant, eminently functional building in which all aspects of design and purpose are perfectly united.

A Home for the Bauhaus

This asymmetric building, which still appears thoroughly modern, was his manifesto in concrete, steel and glass. According to the 1919 manifesto of the Bauhaus, the aim was to have artists, designers, architects, sculptors and painters working together at the school in order to develop the "new buildings of the future".

   The building has three linked L-shaped wings. The workshop wing, which bears the vertical name "Bauhaus" in large letters, is notable for its glass curtain-wall, a feature that gave it the popular name "the Aquarium". This leads directly to a low building where kitchens, canteen and gymnasium are located; and this in turn leads to the much higher accommodation block, on which there's a roof-garden. Linking these blocks with the large Schools of Arts and Crafts is a two-story bridge wing that passes over a road. This wing became the School of Architecture. Unlike the workshop, with its glass wall, this connecting wing and the School of Arts and Crafts have long horizontal rows of windows, and are of a light colour. The windows in the accommodation wing have small balconies. Throughout the complex, interior features and fittings were designed down to the last detail. Purpose built as a school of art and design, the Bauhaus building embodies the groundbreaking ideas of Gropius and his school – a building in which art, craft and modern technology work in harmony. The result was one of the most influential buildings of 20th-century architecture.

BAUHAUS, DESSAU, GERMANY
1925–26

Walter Gropius

1883 Born 18 May in Berlin
1903–07 Studies at the Technical Universities of Munich and Berlin
1907–10 Works as Peter Behrens' assistant in Berlin
1910 Becomes a freelance designer
1911–13 Redesigns the Fagus Shoe Factory, with Adolf Meyer
1916 Marries Alma Schindler Mahler
1919 Teaches at the University for Fine Arts in Weimar (renamed Bauhaus)
1919–30 Siemensstadt, Berlin
1928 Relinquishes his directorship of the Bauhaus; opens his own office in Berlin
1934 Goes into exile in England
1937 Takes position at Harvard University
1958–63 Pan American Building, New York
1969 Dies 5 July in Boston

A staircase in the Dessau Bauhaus

1888 *Sunflowers*, Vincent van Gogh   **1907** *Les Demoiselles d'Avignon*, Picasso

1883 First petrol-driven automobile,   **1898** USA becomes a   **1914** *The Bottle Dryer* (ready-
Gottlieb Daimler and Carl Benz   world power   made), Marcel Duchamps
                                                                  1914–1918 First World War

REVIVALISM 1840–1895   1840–1895 REVIVALISM   1895–1910 ART NOUVEAU   MODERNISM 1910–1980

| 1840 | 1845 | 1850 | 1855 | 1860 | 1865 | 1870 | 1875 | 1880 | 1885 | 1890 | 1895 | 1900 | 1905 | 1910 | 1915 | 1920 | 1925 |

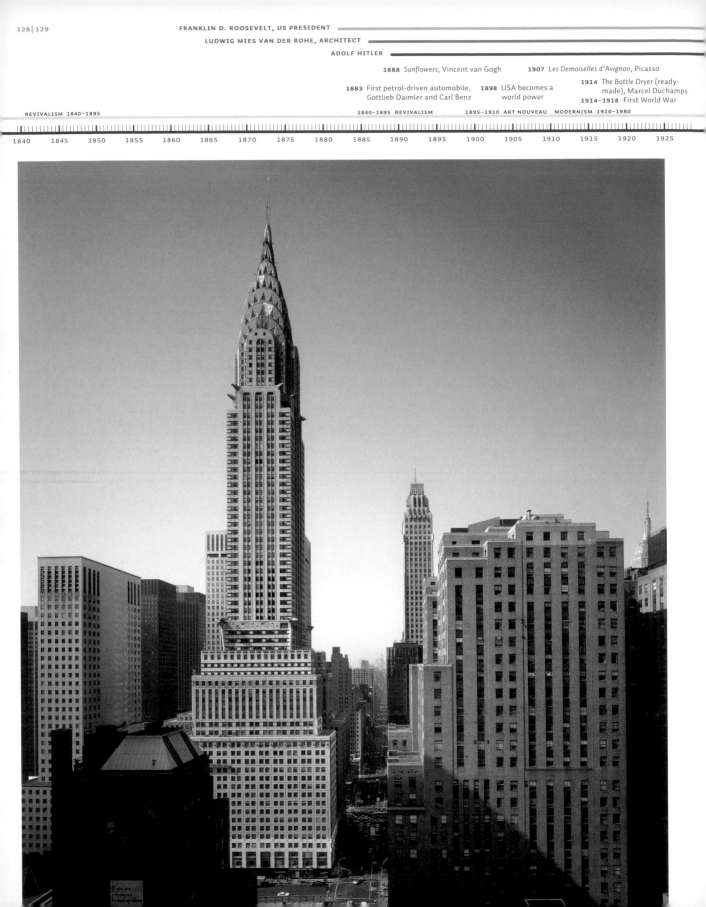

CHRYSLER BUILDING

For a short time, this building was the highest in the world. The urban historian Lewis Mumford said: "Heaven help whoever looks up at this building without being far enough away from it and helped by thick fog." Hard words for the 319-metre (1,050-feet) high Chrysler Building in Manhattan, which started to take shape in October 1928.

Wedding Cake

Three thousand workers laboured in double shifts on the prominent building site opposite the Grand Central Station. Top priority was given to safety and there were no serious accidents during the concentrated building work. First, it was necessary to dig 21 metres (70 feet) into the ground to set the foundations, which have to support 112,000 tons spread over 71 floors. The rectangular base takes up the entire site but the building itself tapers upwards. This "wedding cake style" was widespread in New York in the 1920s, thanks to the new building regulations: it was possible to construct new buildings of great height only if the tower, above the thirteenth floor, took up one-quarter of the area of the base. The aim of the first owner, William H. Reynolds, who soon sold the building to Walter P. Chrysler, was for his new building to surpass the height of the Eiffel Tower in Paris (see pages 122–123) – and he was successful. After some 4,000 windows and almost 3,000 doors had been installed, seven scale-like Art Deco arches were attached to each side of the tower at the top of the building. A steel spire 55 metres (180 feet) long rises out of the tower. In 1931, this spire made the Chrysler Building the highest in the world. But not for long: it was soon surpassed by the Empire State Building, also in New York.

Art Deco

"No old stuff for me. No corrupt copies of gates, columns and oriels. I – I am new! Avanti." The Architect William van Allen was in no way traditional: modern ideas were given priority – from the disposal of garbage in record time, to the radiators recessed in the walls. After William H. Reynolds had handed the project over to the automobile tycoon Walter P. Chrysler, the glittering façade became representative of the mood of the Jazz Age: zigzag patterns, triangles and rectangles of light grey tiles and white marble decorate the building. The metal eagle heads, hubcaps, radiator grilles and other parts reminiscent of cars in the recesses of the building make a clear reference to the man who owned the building. Here, modern technology joined hands with Art Deco to form an extravagant design – the decoration of the exterior of the Chrysler Building was just as important as the decoration of its interior. This approach had its keen admirers: Paul Goldberger, the architecture critic of the *New York Times*, found the building "romantic and irrational, and yet not quite so foolish as to be laughable; it stops just short of that and maintains a bit of credibility in its folly – just like New York itself".

CHRYSLER BUILDING, NEW YORK CITY, USA
1928–30

FACT FILE
Location 405 Lexington Avenue, corner of 42nd Street
Architect William van Alen (1882–1954)
Planning of supporting structure Ralph Squire & Sons
Height 319 m/1,050 ft
Height of steel spire 55 m/180 ft
Total weight Approx. 112,000 tons
Number of storeys 71
Lifts 34
Use Office space

The Chrysler Building was the highest edifice in the world until the Empire State Building was constructed

above:
3,000 workers took part in construction

left:
Lift doors with Art Deco ornaments

right page:
The Chrysler Building – modern technology
and extravagant design

1883 First petrol-driven automobile, Gottlieb Daimler and Carl Benz

1905/1907 Foundation of *Die Brücke* and *Der Blaue Reiter* art groups

1898 USA becomes a world power

1914 *The Bottle Dryer* (readymade), Marcel Duchamps

1914–1918 First World War

REVIVALISM 1840–1895   1840–1895 REVIVALISM   1895–1910 ART NOUVEAU   MODERNISM 1910–1980

| 1850 | 1855 | 1860 | 1865 | 1870 | 1875 | 1880 | 1885 | 1890 | 1895 | 1900 | 1905 | 1910 | 1915 | 1920 | 1925 | 1930 | 1935 |

Casa Malaparte, view from the southwest

below:
View of the property from the cliff path

1952 Elvis Presley becomes popular
1939–1945 Second World War **1960** John F. Kennedy becomes President of the USA
1961 Berlin Wall erected

1910–1980 MODERNISM   POST-MODERNISM FROM 1980

1940   1945   1950   1955   1960   1965   1970   1975   1980   1985   1990   1995   2000   2005   2010   2015   2020   2025

CASA MALAPARTE

Since 1922, building had been forbidden on the east coast of Capri. The authorities were determined that the growing popularity of the small island in the Bay of Naples would not lead to an ugly construction boom. But there was to be an exception.

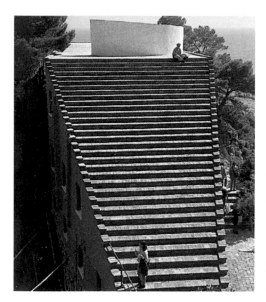

In 1938, a long, red-plastered rectangular building started to take shape on the Punta Massullo. This house juts out to the tip of a bare rock overhang below which the rugged cliff falls steeply into the sea. The Italian authorities had made this single exception for Curzio Malaparte – as the Italian writer and journalist Kurt Erwin Suckert had named himself.

A House as a Portrait
He made his decision the moment he saw the spot. And as it was generally assumed that the plot of land he'd found could not be built on, it was at least very inexpensive. But Curzio Malaparte was well connected to the Fascist Party – and Mussolini's son-in-law in particular – and so he was able to begin construction a mere three months after his arrival on Capri.

Building permission had been given, but it was also necessary to submit the plans drawn up by the architect, Adalberto Libera. His task was not an easy one, for Malaparte never grew tired of stressing his personal authorship of the building. The house on the rocks, he said, was a portrait of himself – all he had needed was "a little help" from a builder on the island. However, it's a matter of record that it was Libera who settled on the basic rectangular form, and on the spectacular open terrace. A staircase, which becomes wider as it ascends, leads up to it. The curious curved concrete wall on the roof, which is plastered white, forms an effective contrast to the warm red of the rest of the house. Its purpose was to provide shelter from the fierce sun. It's also said that Malaparte like to ride his bicycle on the roof – perhaps he also wanted to prevent the curious from seeing him.

A Beautiful Setting
The Casa Malaparte offers many fine views. The differently sized windows are placed asymmetrically along the walls and allow countless views of the countryside and sea to be seen from the interior. The living room, covering more than 100 square metres (1,070 square feet) on the second floor of the low building, occupies most of the area of the house. There are also plenty of guest rooms, and in spite of – or maybe because of – the remote location, many visitors did indeed come to Casa Malaparte. One of them was the film director Jean-Luc Godard, who in 1963 chose the house as the setting for his film *Le Mépris* (Contempt), which starred Brigitte Bardot and Michel Piccoli.

Malaparte himself, once condemned as a Fascist, later made headlines once again. In old age, he turned to Communism and left the house on the fisherman's island to the communist Chinese government in gratitude for their hospitality during his stay in China. Malaparte's relatives contested the will and were ultimately successful.

CASA MALAPARTE, CAPRI, ITALY
1938–43

Adalberto Libera

1903 Born 16 July in Villa Lagarina, Province of Trento
1923–25 Studies at the National Institute of Art in Parma
1925–27 Studies in Rome
1928 Publishes the manifesto *Arte e razionalismo* and participates in the first exhibition of Rationalist architecture in Rome
1931 Holiday resort Porto Civitanova Marche
1932 Jubilee Exhibition of the Fascist Revolution in Rome
1933/34 Post office on the Aventine Hill in Rome
1935 Italian pavilion at the World Exposition in Brussels
1938–43 Casa Malaparte, Capri
1953 Becomes Professor of Design at the faculty of architecture, Florence University
1956–59 Cathedral, La Spezia
1957–60 Olympic Village, Rome
1959 Pharmaceutical laboratory, Latina
1963 Dies 17 March in Rome

A widening staircase leads upwards to the open roof terrace

1898 USA becomes a world power

1914 *The Bottle Dryer* (readymade), Marcel Duchamps
1914–1918 First World War

1939–1945 Second World War

REVIVALISM 1840–1895   1840–1895 REVIVALISM   1895–1910 ART NOUVEAU   MODERNISM 1910–1980

1860   1865   1870   1875   1880   1885   1890   1895   1900   1905   1910   1915   1920   1925   1930   1935   1940   1945

The Glass House – nature forms the borders of the building

"Flowing rooms" without supporting walls

1960 John F. Kennedy becomes President of the USA

1952 Elvis Presley
becomes popular

1962 *One Hundred Cans*, Andy Warhol

1964 USA starts Vietnam War

1950 Beginning of the Korean War

1910–1980 MODERNISM   POST-MODERNISM FROM 1980

1950   1955   1960   1965   1970   1975   1980   1985   1990   1995   2000   2005   2010   2015   2020   2025   2030   2035

THE GLASS HOUSE

The architect Philip Johnson's glass house stands on a broad expanse of lawn surrounded by high, isolated trees. The unpretentious building looks less like a dwelling than a glass box, and seems to enhance or frame the land-scape rather than to intrude upon it.

Philip Johnson had made a name for himself mainly as a theoretician. As head of the architecture department of the New York Museum of Modern Art, he published the catalogue *The International Style: Architecture Since 1922*, together with Henry-Russell Hitchcock, for an exhibition of the same name. They were attempting to find common char-acteristics of modern European architecture, such as the elimination of any ornamentation. Johnson was to carry this to the extreme with the radical simplicity of his own house.

Walls? Forget them!

But first, and now already in his mid-thirties, he started studying architecture. Walter Gropius, the influential Bauhaus architect, was one of his pro-fessors (see pages 126–127). This could not remain without consequences for the budding architect; and when Johnson began constructing his own house in Connecticut in 1947 he set new standards in minimalism. One looks for walls in vain: nature

itself seems to set the boundaries of the building – the supporting steel frame is hardly visible, and all the surfaces between the frames are of uninter-rupted glass. A brick cylinder is the only opaque element: this houses the technical installations and the bathroom. Its red form rises a little above the flat roof and is the only – and very discreet – spot of colour in the one-space house, which is completely assimilated into its surroundings.

Mies van der Johnson

Steel and glass were the two materials that made it possible for architects to dematerialise their build-ings to the extent that there is hardly any perception of an enclosed space. A few years previously, the architect Mies van der Rohe had investigated the concept of "flowing spaces", rooms without any walls. Johnson modelled his building on van der Rohe's glass Farnsworh House, in Illinois. He had recently devoted an exhibition in MoMA to the German-born architect and, in the 1950s, they were jointly to build the New York Seagram Building, a landmark in modern architecture. Some found this degree of co-operation a little curious, and for a while Philip Johnson was nicknamed "Mies van der Johnson". His glass house design, however, did have its admirers, and this generously laid-out house, flooded with light, was admired by many architects, designers and even clients.

THE GLASS HOUSE, NEW CANAAN, USA
1947–49

Philip Cortelyou Johnson

1906 Born 8 July in Cleveland
1927 Graduates in philology at Harvard
1930 Founds the Architecture and Design Department of the Museum of Modern Art, New York
1932 Publishes *The International Style: Architecture Since 1922*, with Henry-Russell Hitchcock
1940 Begins to study architecture (teachers include Walter Gropius and Marcel Breuer)
1946–54 Head of the Architecture Department of the Museum of Modern Art
1947–50 Glass House, New Canaan
1954–58 Seagram Building, New York (concept: Mies van der Rohe)
1967 Begins collaboration with John Burgee
1979 Wins Pritzker Prize
1980–84 AT&T Headquarters, New York
1988 Co-organizes *Deconstructivist Architecture* exhibition
1995 Gate House, New Canaan
2005 Dies 12 September in New Canaan

International Style

During the 1930s and 1940s, many buildings were characterised by simple geometrical forms, such as white cubes, arranged asymmetrically, with windows set in horizontal bands. In 1932, Philip C. Johnson and Henry-Russell Hitchcock devoted an exhibition, *The International Style: Architecture Since 1922*, to this style. The proponents of this movement focused on the functional, and largely ignored the decorative aspects of design. This style is clearly seen in the buildings of Mies van der Rohe, who is generally considered to be the father of the International Style. It spread from the United States to South America, Europe and Asia – it was indeed international. Other impor-tant representatives of the style were Walter Gropius and Le Corbusier (see pages 126–127 and 136–139).

1907 *Les Demoiselles d'Avignon*, Picasso

1914 *The Bottle Dryer* (readymade),   **1939–1945** Second
Marcel Duchamps   World War
1914–1918 First World War

REVIVALISM 1840–1895   1840–1895 REVIVALISM   1895–1910 ART NOUVEAU   MODERNISM 1910–1980

1860   1865   1870   1875   1880   1885   1890   1895   1900   1905   1910   1915   1920   1925   1930   1935   1940   1945

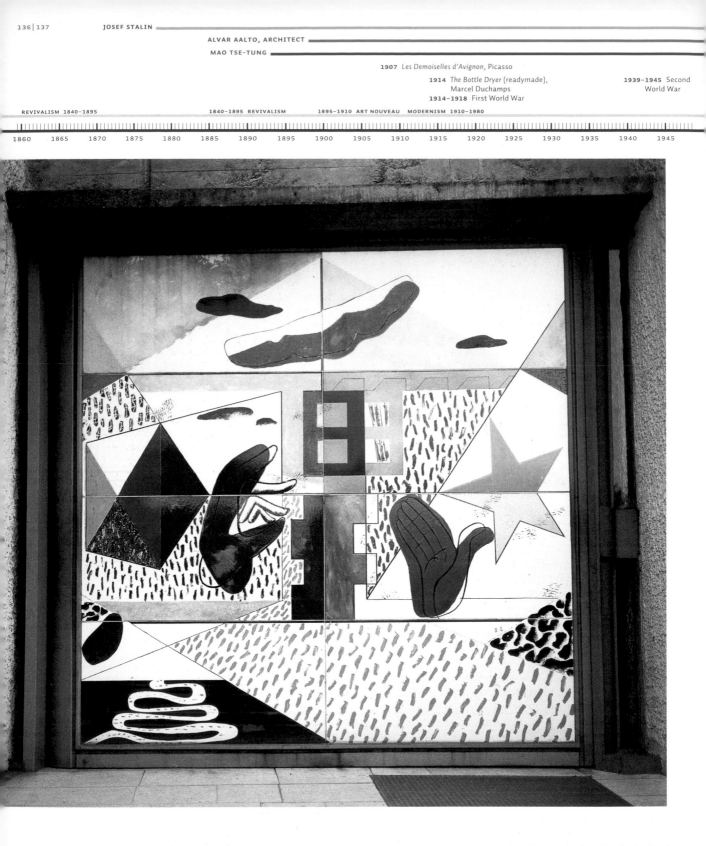

The main entrance of the church is faced
with enamelled steel sheets

1950 Start of the Korean War **1973** First oil crisis

1959 Jean-Luc Godard's film *Breathless* **1961** Berlin Wall erected

1964 USA starts the Vietnam War

1962 *One Hundred Cans*, Andy Warhol

1910–1980 MODERNISM   POST-MODERNISM FROM 1980

| 1950 | 1955 | 1960 | 1965 | 1970 | 1975 | 1980 | 1985 | 1990 | 1995 | 2000 | 2005 | 2010 | 2015 | 2020 | 2025 | 2030 | 2035 |

NOTRE DAME DU HAUT

The local press condemned Le Corbusier's plans for this chapel as "religious rubbish", and as looking like a "slipper". This was no surprise: nowhere was there a sign of a right-angle, a straight side or symmetrical façade. Nevertheless, the chapel of Notre Dame du Haut has long since changed from being a "pile of concrete" into an architectural icon.

"A pilgrimage chapel? It's an arithmetical problem dealing with volumes and quantities!" The architect's enthusiasm for his new commission was not immediate. It was only after the clients had presented convincing arguments that Le Corbusier declared himself prepared to tackle the task, and he was given a free hand in creating a new chapel to take the place of its destroyed predecessor. The celebrated architect was fascinated by two aspects of the project: on the one hand, the harmony between the architecture and the landscape; and, on the other, the complicated requirements of a chapel. A small church for 200 was needed which, twice a year, would become a place of pilgrimage. On 8 September and 15 August, thousands of pilgrims take part in Marian celebrations on the hill above the village of Ronchamp about 20 kilometres (12 miles) from Belfort. The old chapel on the hill witnessed the largest number of pilgrims in 1873, when more than 30,000 believers celebrated the birth of the Virgin Mary – and the end of the Franco-Prussian War – there.

Function and Form

Lying at a height of around 500 metres (1,640 feet) above sea level, the plateau on which the chapel stands provides a secure site in the midst of the green, gently rolling landscape. A chapel had been built there during the Middle Ages. The new chapel, erected between 1950 and 1954, is usually approached from the south: the first sight is of a windowless tower and a protruding, heavy roof resting on a curved white wall. The main entrance, framed on both sides by enamelled steel sheets, is inserted into a straight section of the wall. Le Corbusier was also a painter of abstract pictures and he himself created the design for the main portal. Its lively colours form a contrast to the white plaster. The variously sized window openings seem to be distributed arbitrarily over the outer wall, making it appear to be riddled with holes (their distribution is reminiscent of abstract art). The roof ends at the south-east corner in an upward sweep that suggest the bow of a ship. The external choir, for open-air masses, lies in front of the east wall and is protected by a widely protruding roof. The north wall is dominated by right angles, whereas the western wall is a rounded, windowless surface. The chapel under the brown roof is a dazzling white, but several other sections, such as the pulpit of the external choir and the wall of the entrance portal, are left in bare concrete, as is the pilgrims' hostel with its dormitories and dining rooms, and the custodian's house for the church's chaplain.

NOTRE DAME DU HAUT, RONCHAMP, FRANCE
1950–54

Le Corbusier

1887 Born Charles-Édouard Jeanneret in La-Chaux-de-Fonds in Switzerland
1908/09 Works with the Frères Perret in Paris
1910 Collaborates with Peter Behrens in Berlin
1925 Pavillon de l'Esprit Nouveau at the World Exposition in Paris
1927 Citrohan Haus, Stuttgart
1947–52 Housing settlement Unité d'Habitation in Marseilles
1950–54 Notre Dame du Haut, Ronchamp
1951–56 Chandigarh in northern India is developed following his plans
1953–61 Extension of the La Tourette Monastery in Eveux-sur-Arbresle near Lyon
1963 Carpenter Art Center, Harvard, USA
1965 Dies in Cap-Martin, southern France

Plan from 1951

left:
Notre Dame du Haut, pilgrimage
church and architectural icon

above:
Light flows into the room through
window openings of varying sizes

MAO TSE-TUNG

JOHN F. KENNEDY

JAMES STIRLING, ARCHITECT

1914 *The Bottle Dryer* (readymade),
Marcel Duchamps
1914–1918 First World War

1950 Start of the
Korean War

1939–1945 Second World War

1840–1895 REVIVALISM   **1895–1910 ART NOUVEAU**   **MODERNISM 1910–1980**

1870	1875	1880	1885	1890	1895	1900	1905	1910	1915	1920	1925	1930	1935	1940	1945	1950	1955

The horizontally organized round
construction

1962 *One Hundred Cans, Andy Warhol*   **1973** First oil crisis

1964 USA starts Vietnam War   **1981** First flight of the space-shuttle *Columbia*

1969 Woodstock Music Festival:
400,000 visitors

1910–1980 MODERNISM   POST-MODERNISM FROM 1980

| 1960 | 1965 | 1970 | 1975 | 1980 | 1985 | 1990 | 1995 | 2000 | 2005 | 2010 | 2015 | 2020 | 2025 | 2030 | 2035 | 2040 | 2045 |

GUGGENHEIM MUSEUM

A spiral ramp rising over a circular floor plan hardly suggests a museum. However, the Guggenheim Museum, which was completed in 1959, is now one of the most famous museum buildings in the world.

In 1943, museum curator Hilla Rebay contacted the architect Frank Lloyd Wright. At the time, the collection of modern art the industrialist Solomon Guggenheim had accumulated was without a suitable exhibition space: "I need a warrior, a lover of space, an organizer, an experimental and wise man … I want a temple of the spirit, a monument", was how the project was explained to the architect. For Wright, the location in New York was anything but inspiring; but, on the other hand, he was attracted to the prospect of building a museum. He presented his plans, not knowing that over the next 15 years, six additional plans with more than 700 drawings would be required.

Architecture as Sculpture

In 1945, the architect and client were in broad agreement, but the economic situation in post-war America meant that things moved very slowly. Not only that: Frank Lloyd Wright had to search for a long time before finding the right builder in George Cohen, who was prepared to undertake avant-garde projects – for the building, which would stand on Fifth Avenue between 88th and 89th Streets, was a radically new design. In essence, it's a pile of round discs that increase in diameter as the building rises. What Frank Lloyd Wright created in the heart of Manhattan, not far from Central Park, was in effect a walk-in sculpture.

What about the Art?

Everything looks very different on the inside. The round forms become accessible as spirals, and a long ramp winds its way along the external wall from the ground floor to the upper storey. A glass dome provides illumination from above. Wright even had advice for visitors: they should take a lift to the very top and then wander down, step by slow step, through the entire collection.

The building was not immediately convincing: critics thought that the art by Kandinsky, Klee and Chagall would be overpowered by the building itself. Willem de Kooning and other artists asked themselves – and the public – how their works could be shown on the curved walls of such an unusual building. However, Wright didn't allow himself to be deterred, even when his building was said to resemble a washing machine: "I have heard so many similar reactions and have decided to simply ignore them." The architect did not live to see the opening of the Guggenheim Museum. Half a year before construction was completed in November 1959, and 16 years after his first sketches, Frank Lloyd Wright died at the age of 92.

GUGGENHEIM MUSEUM, NEW YORK CITY, USA
1956–59

Frank Lloyd Wright

1867 Born in Richland Center, Wisconsin
1887 Begins work in the architectural office of Louis Henry Sullivan and Dankmar Adler, in Chicago
ca. 1900 Prairie Houses in the suburbs of Chicago
1916–20 Hotel Imperial in Tokyo (destroyed), together with Antonin Raymond
1920s Private houses in California, using prefabricated concrete modules
1935/36 Falling Water House in Bear Run, Pennsylvania
1936–39 Johnson Administration Building in Racine, Wisconsin
1956–59 Guggenheim Museum, New York
1959 Dies in Phoenix, Arizona

above:
The spiral ramp winds its way upwards
to the glass cupola

The glass cupola of the round building

Exterior view from Fifth Avenue

1914 *The Bottle Dryer* (readymade),
Marcel Duchamps
1914–1918 First World War

1950 Start of the
Korean War

1939–1945 Second World War

1840–1895 REVIVALISM　　1895–1910 ART NOUVEAU　MODERNISM 1910–1980

| 1870 | 1875 | 1880 | 1885 | 1890 | 1895 | 1900 | 1905 | 1910 | 1915 | 1920 | 1925 | 1930 | 1935 | 1940 | 1945 | 1950 | 1955 |

"The Spirit of Flight" – the TWA Terminal
at John F. Kennedy International Airport

Floor plan

1962	One Hundred Cans, Andy Warhol	1973	First oil crisis
1964	USA starts Vietnam War	1981	First flight of the space-shuttle *Columbia*
1969	Woodstock Music Festival: 400,000 visitors		

1910–1980 MODERNISM   POST-MODERNISM FROM 1980

| 1960 | 1965 | 1970 | 1975 | 1980 | 1985 | 1990 | 1995 | 2000 | 2005 | 2010 | 2015 | 2020 | 2025 | 2030 | 2035 | 2040 | 2045 |

TWA TERMINAL

The idea that sparked his highly original design for the airport terminal came to the Finnish architect Eero Saarinen while he was looking at the leftovers of a grapefruit after breakfast. The inspiration may have been prosaic, but the result was one of his most remarkable and original buildings.

The new terminal for the largest of New York airports, John F. Kennedy International, looks much more like a journey into the future than the fruit. Saarinen was originally a sculptor before devoting his passion for experimentation to architecture. "We wanted the passengers passing through the rooms to feel themselves in an environment where each section is the consequence of the previous one and all originate in the same formal universe." This statement by Saarinen is a little more informative, but it still doesn't say anything about the choice of forms – does the building resemble a gargantuan bird rising into the skies with its outspread wings … or is it more like a larger-than-life predatory fish?

The Spirit of Flight

J.F.K. Airport occupies an area of 20 square kilometres (eight square miles) to the east of New York. Even before Saarinen's terminal was built, the airport had seen designs of great architectural variety, for the terminals of various airlines enlivened the central building. When Trans World Airlines commissioned the Finnish architect, they gave him carte blanche – his plan had convinced them. A concrete dish made of four arches forms the astonishing roof of the building, with rows of windows nestling beneath these "wings". The roof construction is supported by Y-form supports, whose lines continue in the curved lines of the roof bowl. In the 12,000 square metres (129,200 square feet) of the interior, everything – from the desks to the notice boards – seems to be in movement, precisely capturing the character of an airport.

The airline company let the implementation of Saarinen's plans for a building of glass and concrete cost them $15m. Sadly, the architect did not live to see the opening of his terminal; he died almost one year before its completion. Not, however, without leaving a poetic note behind – he had wanted, he said, to capture "the spirit of flight" in his design for the terminal. Saarinen's architectural sculpture could not keep pace with the rapid boom in air transport for very long, however, for the demands placed on the terminal changed soon after its completion. Since 1960, the number of passengers at J.F.K. airport has increased fourfold, which has made a series of alterations to the building necessary. There are limits to change, however: the TWA Terminal was named a protected monument in 1994.

TWA TERMINAL, NEW YORK CITY, USA
1956–62

Eero Saarinen

1910 Born 20 August in Kirkkonumnii, Finland
1923 Settles in the USA
1929–34 Studies in Paris and at Yale University
1951–57 General Motors' Technical Center, Warren, Michigan
1955–59/61 US embassy buildings in Oslo and London
1956–62 TWA Terminal, J.F. Kennedy Airport, New York
1957–61 T.J. Watson Research Center, Yorktown, New York
1958 Hockey Stadium, New Haven, Connecticut
1958–63 Dulles International Airport, Washington, D.C.
1961 Dies 1 September in Ann Arbor
1962 Gold medal of the American Institute of architects

Plastic Style

Where the Bauhaus architects impressed with their simple cubic forms arranged asymmetrically, and with window arranged in horizontal strips, other designers emerged after the Second World War with a very different approach: they focussed on plasticity and monumentality and renounced all ornamental decoration. Concrete was the preferred construction material of these advocates of the "plastic style". Well-known examples include Le Corbusier's pilgrimage chapel in Ronchamp, Oscar Niemeyer's buildings in Brasília, as well as Frank Lloyd Wright's sculptural Guggenheim Museum in New York.

following double page:
One wing of the terminal

1914–1918 First World War   **1939–1945** Second World War

1840–1895 REVIVALISM   **1895–1910 ART NOUVEAU**   **MODERNISM 1910–1980**

1870   1875   1880   1885   1890   1895   1900   1905   1910   1915   1920   1925   1930   1935   1940   1945   1950   1955

The bowl above the House of
Representatives

Urban Planning
Whether used for the development of existing
settlements, or of entirely new developments,
the term "urban planning" was not employed
before the end of the 19th century. Many ancient
cities were characterized by a right-angled system
of streets, the Romans in particular favoured a
regular, grid plan for their towns. In the Middle
Ages, cities were mainly established on former
ancient settlements, which were often irregular in
layout, as well as in the areas around monasteries
and castles. During the Renaissance and the
Baroque there was a new focus on "ideal cities",
with Palmanova in Italy and Mannheim in
Germany being prominent examples. Planned
cities can also be found in modern times:
in addition to Niemeyer's plans for Brasília,
Le Corbusier designed Chandigarh in India.

1962 *One Hundred Cans,*
Andy Warhol

1980 Ronald Reagan becomes
President of the USA

1995 Christo wraps the Berlin Reichstag

1973 First oil crisis

1982 *Fettecke,* Joseph Beuys

1964 USA starts Vietnam War

1986 Space-shuttle *Challenger* explodes in flight

1910–1980 MODERNISM   POST-MODERNISM FROM 1980

1960   1965   1970   1975   1980   1985   1990   1995   2000   2005   2010   2015   2020   2025   2030   2035   2040   2045

CONGRESS BUILDING BRASÍLIA

By the middle of the 20th century, Brazil was well on its way to becoming a modern industrialized nation, a fact that its political leaders felt had to be expressed in its urban architecture. The precise central point of the gigantic country was calculated and a new capital city was planned to emerge just there, on a distant, sparsely populated plateau in the very heart of the country.

In a way, Brasília – a planned city, built of concrete in a tropical climate – was intended to be a kind of welcoming gift for the new President Juscelino Kubitschek de Oliveira. Brasília could not be expected to supplant the lively and well-established old capital, Rio de Janeiro, located 1,000 kilometres (620 miles) away. But, by the year 2000, more than two million inhabitants lived in the new city, which had been planned for only 500,000. Their enthusiasm for the artificially created city, however, has its limits. There is a common saying among Brazilians that the most attractive view of Brasília is seen on the flight to Rio!

Technology and Tempo

The new city is sited at an altitude of 1,150 metres (3,770 feet) above sea level. The urban planners Lucio Costa and Oscar Niemeyer were largely responsible for its development. They began with their plans for the no-man's-land in 1957, and in only three years, 80,000 workers had created the new centre of the country out of nothing – the only demand the President placed on his planning team was the city had to be built as quickly as possible. The city was officially dedicated in 1960.

The remote area had offered the planners one great advantage: they didn't have to take existing buildings or sites into consideration, so it was possible to create something completely new quickly – it's hardly possible to express the belief in progress and technology more clearly. For all its straightforward functionalism, Niemeyer's architecture is rich in symbolism.

Significant Features

"It was always important for me that my buildings have something surprising about them, that they invent something previously unseen." There can be no question that Niemeyer relished the surprising moments in the numerous civic buildings he erected

in a line along the north-south axis. Among these governmental and cultural buildings we find government ministries, the university, the congress building, and its neighbours on the "Square of the Three Forces", the Supreme Court and the presidential palace. A high-rise building housing the representatives' offices towers above a low building that is home to the House of Representatives and the Senate. The scene is dominated by straight lines and right angles, and the façades are sheathed in glass. All very modern. Two huge bowls lie resplendent on the flat roofs: one forms the dome of the Senate (and so suggests containment), the other, upturned and open above, sits on the roof of the House of Representatives (representing a container for the votes of the people). The views of the surrounding country that can be seen from this building are no less impressive.

CONGRESS BUILDING, BRASÍLIA, BRAZIL
1958–60

Oscar Niemeyer

1907 Born 15 December in Rio de Janeiro
1930–34 Studies architecture at the Academy of Fine Arts, Rio de Janeiro
1936–43 Meets Le Corbusier when working on Education Ministry in Rio de Janeiro
1946 Boavista Bank, Rio de Janeiro
1954 Palace of Industry, São Paulo
1956–61 Works as chief architect of Brasília
1964 Goes into exile when military dictatorship comes to power in Brazil
1967 PCF Centre, Paris
1969 Renault headquarters, Paris; Constantine University, Algeria
1978 Theatre and Congress Centre, Venice
1983/84 Samba Stadium in Rio de Janeiro
1988 Wins Pritzker Prize
1989 Cultural Centre, São Paulo
1996 Museum of Modern Art, Rio de Janeiro
2002 Casino in Funchal, Madeira

Ramp to the roof terrace of the
Congress Building with the towers of
the Supreme Administration Authority
in the background

below:
Overall view of the Congress Building

MAO TSE-TUNG

JOHN F. KENNEDY

JAMES STIRLING, ARCHITECT

1914–1918 First World War   **1939–1945** Second World War

1840–1895 REVIVALISM   1895–1910 ART NOUVEAU   MODERNISM 1910–1980

| 1870 | 1875 | 1880 | 1885 | 1890 | 1895 | 1900 | 1905 | 1910 | 1915 | 1920 | 1925 | 1930 | 1935 | 1940 | 1945 | 1950 | 1955 |

The Sydney Opera House, the city's
symbol

1962 One Hundred Cans, Andy Warhol
1964 USA starts Vietnam War
1986 Space-shuttle *Challenger* explodes in flight
1981 First flight of the space-shuttle *Columbia*
1982 *Fettecke*, Joseph Beuys
1989 Berlin Wall opened; collapse of the Communist Eastern Bloc
1995 Christo wraps the Berlin Reichstag

1910–1980 MODERNISM   POST-MODERNISM FROM 1980

1960 1965 1970 1975 1980 1985 1990 1995 2000 2005 2010 2015 2020 2025 2030 2035 2040 2045

SYDNEY OPERA HOUSE

Not far from Sydney, a small peninsula, known as Bennelong Point, juts into the bay. Inspired by this strip of land between city and sea, the Danish architect Jørn Utzon created a highly original and once controversial opera house that soon became the proud symbol of Sydney – a confidently modern image for a city increasingly affluent and cosmopolitan.

When the city announced the competition for an opera house in 1956, the intention was to provide seating for 7,000 people and to have two main halls: a large one for symphonic concerts, opera and ballet, and a smaller one for theatrical performances, chamber music and readings. Utzon, who won the competition from among 222 participants, met these conditions and with a striking design – though from the outside there's no telling precisely what's happening on the inside!

An Opera House as Sculpture

Visitors reach the various halls by climbing broad flights of steps that lead up to the concrete platform of which the complex stands. The smallest of the three "shells" stands over a restaurant. The next in size contains the opera house, and the largest houses both the concert hall and (below that) a small theatre. From the exterior, the shell-like roofs dominate completely. These remarkable structures, reminiscent of shells or sails (both perfectly in keeping with it harbour-side setting), give the building a highly sculpted appearance. Their curved surfaces are covered with large glazed ceramic tiles that shine a brilliant white in the Australian sun.

And Utzon was concerned not just with what the visitor heard, but also with what they saw: the Opera House is located on a platform 15 metres (49 feet) high that provides breathtaking views of the harbour and coastline. The building is surrounded by water on three sides – its closest neighbours are not houses and office blocks but boats and ships.

Risk and Success

The reaction to his winning design could hardly have been more varied, ranging from "sheer poetry" to "a Danish pastr". And it was not only the critical reaction that was a risk: technically, the building pushed the boundaries of what was possible at the time. The leading engineer Ove Orup was responsible for constructing the innovative shell structures. Ten thousand workers from 28 countries worked on the building between 1959 and 1973, and in 1962 Utzon moved to Sydney to oversee progress. And there were problems that had nothing to do with design or the technology. During the turbulent 1960s, various social movements used the most prominent building site in Australia to publicise their demonstrations; the workers went on strike for better conditions and pay; and members of the ecological movement challenged the project's environmental impact on the bay.

But construction progressed and the roof was completed in 1967. However, Utzon was back in his

SYDNEY OPERA HOUSE, AUSTRALIA
1957–73

Jørn Utzon

1918 Born 9 April in Copenhagen
1942 Completes his architecture studies at the Copenhagen Academy of Arts
1946 Works with Alvar Aalto in Helsinki
1947/48 Travels through Europe, Morocco and Mexico
1950 Becomes a freelance architect
1956 Wins international attention with his prize-winning plans for the Sydney Opera House
1959 Melli Bank, Teheran
1963 Museum in Silkeborg, Denmark
1983 Parliament Building in Kuwait
2003 Wins Pritzker Prize

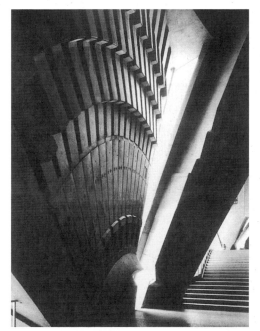

Fan-like wall decoration in the interior

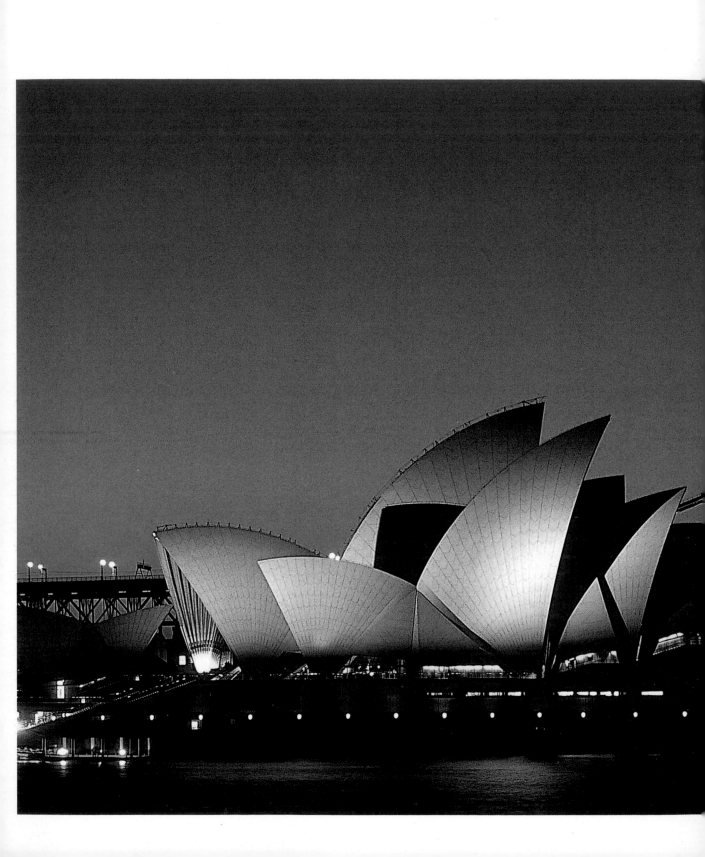

distant homeland by this stage. One year before, he had withdrawn from the project and returned to Denmark – costs had skyrocketed since construction had begun and Utzon was in a catastrophic financial situation. His successors completed work on the building in 1973. It was not until 2000 that Utzon – then 82 – finally accepted the Australian government's request to continue working on the upkeep and improvement of the interior of his masterpiece.

The Opera House is located on a small tongue of land between the harbour and the city centre

JOHN F. KENNEDY

1929– FRANK GEHRY, ARCHITECT

1931– MIKHAIL GORBACHEV

1962 *One Hundred Cans,*
Andy Warhol

1964 USA starts
Vietnam War

1914–1918 First World War   **1939–1945** Second World War

REVIVALISM   1895–1910 ART NOUVEAU   MODERNISM 1910–1980   1910–1980 MODERNISM

1890   1895   1900   1905   1910   1915   1920   1925   1930   1935   1940   1945   1950   1955   1960   1965   1970   1975

above:
The roof landscape of the Olympic Park
quotes the shoreline of the Olympic Lake

below:
The tent-roof construction, transparent
and light

1981 First flight of the space-shuttle *Columbia*   2003 Third Gulf War (US invasion of Iraq)
1982 *Fettecke*,
     Joseph Beuys   1995 Christo wraps the Berlin Reichstag
           1989 Berlin Wall opened; collapse of the Communist Eastern Bloc

POST-MODERNISM FROM 1980

1980   1985   1990   1995   2000   2005   2010   2015   2020   2025   2030   2035   2040   2045   2050   2055   260   2065

OLYMPIC PARK IN MUNICH

"Faster, higher, stronger?" A definite "deeper!" was added to this sporting motto for the Olympic Games in Munich in 1972 – two-thirds of the Olympic Stadium is located underground in a deep depression in the landscape.

A park landscape with no intrusive buildings was the aim for Munich. Those who commissioned the stadium wanted an Olympic Games in the country-side. The intention was to create a counterpart to the Olympic Stadium in Berlin, where the Games in 1936 were used primarily as a demonstration of political power. So to avoid too powerful an impression, only one-third of the Munich Olympic Stadium was erected above ground; two-thirds was built below the surface. The challenge of working with a limited number of materials was met with the curved roof that quickly became the symbol of the 1972 Summer Olympics.

The "Tent"

The ultramodern "net construction" technique that made it possible to span large areas had emerged in the 1950s, and the engineer Frei Otto developed the membrane structure further. At Munich, the net of translucent acrylic glass sheets, which measures a vast 74,800 square metres (805,140 square feet), forms a tent-like structure that stretches over the landscape and buildings, the western section of the Olympic Stadium, the Olympic Hall, and the swimming arena. This roof is supported by only 12 pylons, the highest of which measures 81 metres (266 feet),

and 36 smaller round supports. This is possible because the weight is carried by steel cables and cement blocks set deep into the ground.

Not all experts were convinced that the design would work, as they considered the enormous span of the net construction "tent" to be far too large. But it was successful, though there was one problem: the covering of the roof cost ten times the original (already substantial) estimate! The issue was hotly debated by the chief architect, Günter Behnisch, and the Olympic Building Consortium (OBG), which consisted of the federal government and the state government. To his claim that he had "designed a Volkswagen and the OBG turned it into a Cadillac", they replied that "Behnisch planned a Cadillac and thought he could power it with a Volkswagen engine".

Today

Whether a Cadillac or a Volkswagen, the Olympic Park, which was laid out in northern Munich between 1968 and 1972, is still in use today. Covering three square kilometres (1.2 square miles), this large recreational area is now used for numerous sporting and cultural events. It's no problem to climb the 60 metres (197 feet) of the Olympic Hill, but the 290 metres (950 feet) of the Olympia Tower – the highest reinforced concrete construction in Europe – is more demanding. The Nymphenburg Canal was turned into the Olympia Lake, and the Stadium, with its 57,450 seats and standing room for 12,000, is used for concerts today. Moreover, the former Olympic Village has become home to around 9,000 residents.

This former parade ground, which was later used as Munich's first airport, and even as a dump for rubble after the Second World War, has finally become an integral part of the city's landscape.

OLYMPIC PARK, MUNICH, GERMANY
1968–72

Günter Behnisch

1922 Born in Lockwitz near Dresden
1947–51 Studies architecture at the Technical University in Stuttgart
1952 Sets up an architectural studio with Bruno Lambart
1967–72 Olympic Park, Munich
1973–80 Reconstruction of the Schlossplatz (Castle Square) and Königsstrasse in Stuttgart
1987 Library of the Catholic University, Eichstätt
1990 Museum for Post and Communication, Frankfurt am Main
1992 Bundestag Building, Bonn
2001 Buchheim Museum Bernried

JOHN F. KENNEDY

1929– FRANK GEHRY, ARCHITECT

1931– MIKHAIL GORBACHEV

1939–1945 Second World War

1962 One Hundred Cans,
Andy Warhol

1964 USA starts
Vietnam War

REVIVALISM   1895–1910 ART NOUVEAU   MODERNISM 1910–1980   1910–1980 MODERNISM

1890   1895   1900   1905   1910   1915   1920   1925   1930   1935   1940   1945   1950   1955   1960   1965   1970   1975

Zinc sheets and slit-like rows of windows
characterize the external appearance of
the Museum

1981 First flight of the space-shuttle *Columbia*
1982 Fettecke,
Joseph Beuys
1989 Berlin Wall opened; collapse of the Communist Eastern Bloc
1995 Christo wraps the Berlin Reichstag
2003 Third Gulf War (US invasion of Iraq)
2004 Tsunami in Asia claims around 231,000 victims

POST-MODERNISM FROM 1980

1980   1985   1990   1995   2000   2005   2010   2015   2020   2025   2030   2035   2040   2045   2050   2055   260   2065

JEWISH MUSEUM BERLIN

Daniel Libeskind was already a professional musician when his interest in architecture awoke. The extension to the museum to commemorate 2,000 years of German-Jewish history, which he built in the Berlin suburb of Kreuzberg, was his first major project – and it proved controversial and deeply moving.

Seen from the outside, the Jewish Museum consists of two very different buildings. The visitor is initially greeted by a Baroque, three-winged building in cheerful yellow. This two-storey building was erected in 1730 by Johann Philipp Gerlach, and originally served as a courthouse under Frederick William I. Since 2001, it has been part of the research and documents centre on Jewish history. Commissioned for the Museum's permanent exhibition, the new building, with its stark, irregular metallic forms, stands out strongly against its elegant Baroque neighbour.

Between the Lines

This ultra-modern extension, built on a zigzag ground plan, is covered with silver-grey sheets of zinc and is cut open with a series of slit-like windows. Designed by Daniel Libeskind, this building, which is connected to the older one by an underground flight of stairs, is initially very perplexing to its many visitors, for the more familiar arrangement of rooms and passageways has been abandoned. Some of the floors slope, there are strangely angled corners, and many areas are in semi-darkness. Libeskind wanted to create what he called underground "streets", a series of passageways, each leading to a different part of the building. Even the shell of the building attracted masses of visitors: 350,000 visited the still-empty building. Since then, more than 3.5 million visitors have wandered through the tortuous structure.

"The official name of the project is 'Jewish Museum', but I called it 'Between the Lines', because, in my opinion, we are dealing with two lines, two flows of consciousness, organization and connections. One line is straight, but split into many fragments, the other winds its way and continues on eternally", was how the architect described it.

Rich in Symbolism

At the point where these two lines meet there are five empty spaces called "Voids", which, with their naked concrete walls, represent the emptiness left by the Holocaust. The subterranean passageways lead to the various main areas of the exhibition. The first and longest of the three is the "Axis of Continuity", which leads steeply upwards into the two floors of the permanent exhibition. The "Axis of Emigration", on the other hand, guides the visitor to the outside along a corridor that becomes increasingly narrow between its slightly slanting walls. In an underground garden, there is an area containing 49 huge white pillars, filled with earth, out of which trees grow. The third axis, the "Axis of the Holocaust", draws the visitor into a dark passage in which there is a heavy steel door that closes with a heavy thud: behind this lies the 24-metre (79-feet) high Holocaust Tower – a cold, dark, completely empty space dedicated to the memory of the Jewish victims of the Holocaust.

**JEWISH MUSEUM BERLIN,
GERMANY**
1992–99

Daniel Libeskind

1946 Born in Poland
1965 Granted American citizenship
Studies music in Israel and New York
1970 Completes his architectural studies at the Cooper Union for the Advancement of Science and Art in New York
1989 Wins the competition for the construction of the Jewish Museum Berlin
1995–98 Felix Nussbaum Haus, City Museum Osnabrück
1999 Wins German Architectural Prize for the Jewish Museum
2003 Wins the competition for the World Trade Center site at Ground Zero in New York
Currently: Extension of the Denver Art Museum, Creative Media Center in Hong Kong, Military Museum Dresden, and other projects

left page:
One of the three axes

right:
View of the Lindenstrasse façade

below:
The Garden of Steles

JOHN F. KENNEDY

1929– FRANK GEHRY, ARCHITECT

1931– MIKHAIL GORBACHEV

1939–1945 Second World War

1962 One Hundred Cans,
Andy Warhol

1964 USA starts
Vietnam War

REVIVALISM   1895–1910 ART NOUVEAU   MODERNISM 1910–1980   1910–1980 MODERNISM

1890   1895   1900   1905   1910   1915   1920   1925   1930   1935   1940   1945   1950   1955   1960   1965   1970   1975

A bird's eye view of the Olympic Stadium

Net-like construction: Façade and load-bearing structure are one and the same

1981 First flight of the space-shuttle *Columbia*   **2003** Third Golf War (US invasion of Iraq)
1982 *Fettecke,*   **2004** Tsunami in Asia claims around 231,000 victims
         Joseph Beuys   **1995** Christo wraps the Berlin Reichstag
1989 Berlin Wall opened; collapse of the Communist Eastern Bloc

POST-MODERNISM FROM 1980

| 1980 | 1985 | 1990 | 1995 | 2000 | 2005 | 2010 | 2015 | 2020 | 2025 | 2030 | 2035 | 2040 | 2045 | 2050 | 2055 | 260 | 2065 |

NATIONAL STADIUM IN BEIJING

It's expected that 91,000 spectators will be able to view the sporting events presented in Beijing's Olympic Stadium, the "Bird's Nest". This spectacular arena for the 29th Summer Olympic Games, which will be held in 2008, was designed by the Swiss architects Herzog & de Meuron, in collaboration with local Chinese architects.

The Olympic Games in Beijing (Peking) have provided many opportunities to create spectacular new and innovative buildings; the challenge is how to integrate them into the existing city. Following the master plan by Sasaki Associates, who won the competition to develop the Olympic Site, the sporting facilities will flank the axis that runs through the Chinese capital – from Forest Park in the north, past the Forbidden City, to Tiananmen Square in the south – thereby linking nature, sport and culture. The northern end of the axis forms the core area for the Games. Here the buildings are embedded in generous green areas, hills, woods and biotopes, and the city landscape is interspersed with numerous pools and lakes. Work on the new Olympic Stadium began in 2003, around the cube-shaped swimming centre.

The "Bird's Nest"
The design for the stadium was nicknamed the "bird's nest" at the very beginning, the name greatly appealing to the Swiss architects. They describe their office as a laboratory where the "processes of nature are imitated". They employ 240 professionals from 25 countries who work on 40 parallel projects. And indeed this remarkable structure, a vast bowl, does resemble a bird's nest. For the architects, it satisfies four conditions: it's a fully contemporary Chinese building, it exploits the advantages of modern technology, it respects its natural environment, and it has close links with traditional Chinese culture. The longitudinal axis extends over 320 metres (1,049 feet) and the width is 297.3 metres (975 feet). This monumental bird's nest sits raised on a base platform that made it possible to do without excavating a foundation.

Who Needs a Roof?
This remarkable building consists of long, interwoven members that create a vast, net-like structure that it self-supporting. In the same way

as birds line their nests with material, the architects have closed the open surfaces of the exterior with a transparent membrane that allows for ventilation. In this design, façade and structure are identical. The fact that this structure is self-supporting means that there are no pillars in the 69-metre (226-feet) high interior to prevent the sporting fans from having an unobstructed view of their sporting heroes – the field of vision is unrestricted in all directions.

Just a year after they had begun, the architects had to abandon the original plan to cover the interior entirely with a transparent sliding roof. The costs had already greatly exceeded early estimates. However, the new roof design will also provide a worthy covering for the track-and-field events, the football tournament and, of course, the elaborate opening and closing ceremonies of the Olympics in the Far East.

NATIONAL STADIUM, BEIJING, CHINA
2003–08

Architects:
Herzog & de Meuron, Basel, Switzerland
Engineering and Sports Architecture:
China Architectural Design & Research Group, Beijing, China
Ove Arup & Partners Hong Kong Ltd., Kowloon, Hong Kong
Arup Sports, London, United Kingdom
Artistic Consultation:
Ai Weiwei, Beijing, China

Jacques Herzog & Pierre de Meuron

1950 Both born in Basel
1970–75 Study Architecture at the Federal Institute of Technology (ETH) Zurich
1978 Start their collaboration
1987 Ricola Warehouse, Laufen
1992 Goetz Collection, collection of contemporary art in Munich
1998 Dominus Winery, Yountville
SINCE 1999 Professorship at the ETH, Zurich
2000 Tate Modern, London
2001 Win Pritzker Prize. Fünf Höfe (Five Courtyards), Munich
2002 Co-founded ETH Studio Basel – City of the Present Institute, Basel
2003 Prada Aoyama Epicenter, Tokyo. Schaulager Laurenz-Foundation, Basel. Laban Creekside, London
2004 Forum 2004, Barcelona. IKMZ BTU, Cottbus
2005 Allianz Arena, Munich, Walker Art Center, Minneapolis. de Young Museum, San Francisco
2007 National Stadium for the Olympic Games 2008, Beijing. Caixa Forum-Madrid.
2010 Elbphilharmonie, Hamburg

A transparent membrane allows for the open spaces to be sealed

APPENDIX

GLOSSARY

Art Deco
A decorative style of the 1920s and 1930s, characterised by elegant but simple forms (in contrast to the linear richness of Art Nouveau), bold colours and the use of precious materials such as lacquer, ivory, marble, chrome etc. It was named after an exhibition of applied arts held in Paris in 1925.

Basilica
(Greek basilikḗ: "king's hall") In antiquity, a grand, hall-like public building consisting of a long central section (nave) flanked by two isles that are separated from the nave by rows of columns. The nave is wider and considerably higher than the two side aisles. The basilica became one of the most important forms of early Christian and mediaeval church building. In its church form, an altar niche (the apse) is usually attached to the eastern end of the nave.

Central-plan Building
A building in which the main axes radiate from a central point. This means that the possible layouts are circular, oval, square, cross-shaped, octagonal or polygonal. The central room can be surrounded by a gallery and/or open onto chapels, niches and other adjacent rooms. One of the oldest preserved central-plan buildings is the Pantheon in Rome.

Choir
The altar area at the east end of a church, originally reserved for the clergy. Initially separated from the rest of the church by a chancel screen, over time it developed its own distinctive architectural form and decoration (such as choir stalls). Among its special features are the ambulatory (an extension of the side aisles around the choir) and choir chapels.

Column
A perpendicular building support (of wood, stone or metal) with a round cross-section – this distinguishes it from half-columns, pillars and pilasters. In contrast to a pillar, a column does not necessarily play a structural role: it can be merely decorative. Columns can also be free-standing monument: a well-known example is Nelson's Column in London. A column's structure and decoration are based on the three main classical forms: Doric, Ionic and Corinthian. See below.

Corinthian Column
The last of the three classical orders to develop, and the most elaborate. Its base and shaft are generally similar to those of the Ionic column (see next page). The biggest differences are found in the capital: the number of volutes topping the capital is increased from two to eight, but they are greatly reduced in size and seldom project far over the side of the column. The scrolls grow out of stylized acanthus leaves arranged in two rows, one above the other.

Cornice
A decorative moulding designed to mark the transitions between the horizontal sections of a building. They are typically found on an entablature, a wall (usually high up), the point where a wall and roof meet, over a window or door, and on a pedestal.

Doric Column
The oldest (and simplest) of the three classical architectural orders. In contrast to the Ionic and Corinthian orders, the Doric column has no base, which means that the column begins immediately with its shaft, which is fluted (decorated with vertical grooves) and is thicker than those of an Ionic or Corinthian columns. The capital is small, plain and round, and crowned with a square slab called an abacus.

Frieze
Initially part of the entablature in Greek temple, a frieze late became a long, horizontal band on a wall, internal or external, carrying painted or carved ornaments or figural representations. Architecturally, a frieze serves to articulate a large expanse of wall.

Giant (or Colossal) Order
A classical building design in which columns, pillars or pilasters stretch over two or more storeys. The Colossal order was used to make a façade far more impressive.

Ionic Column

One of the three classical architectural orders, more ornate than Doric but simpler than Corinthian. The foundation is formed by a square base plate (plinth) on which rests several rounded bands. The column itself is fluted, and the capital is often formed by a horizontal band of finely carved decoration that sits between two large volutes scrolling down on each side.

Neo-Classicism

A style in art and architecture, flourishing c. 1770–1840, that was a reaction to the light, playful, organic forms of the Rococo period. Based on a return to the architecture of classical antiquity, it employed characteristic elements of Greek and Roman design, notably columns, pediments and porticoes. The emphasis was on order, proportion, a restrained grandeur and a sometimes austere simplicity. By the middle of the 18th century, Italy – and Rome in particular – had become the source of inspiration for artists, architects, writers and political thinkers. The Brandenburg Gate in Berlin, the Arc-de-Triomphe in Paris, the British Museum in London, and the Capitol in Washington are among the most famous Neo-Classical buildings.

Latin Cross

A cross in which a long vertical beam is intersected by a shorter crossbeam above the centre. This is the basic form of most Christian churches: a long nave intersected by short transepts.

Loggia

(Italian: "columned hall") A part of a building open on at least one side, which, in contrast to the portico or balcony, does not protrude beyond the building's profile. The open sides are often supported by slender columns. Loggias were particularly popular in the palaces of the Italian Renaissance.

Mannerism

The dominant style of the period between the Renaissance and Baroque in painting, architecture, sculpture, music and literature, c. 1520–1620. The term was introduced by Giorgio Vasari in reference to Michelangelo ("maniera di Michelangelo"). It is characterised by the renunciation of the harmonious and balanced compositions of the Renaissance in favour of tense, expressive works full of emotion, unrest and exaggerated elegance. The Escorial near Madrid is an important architectural example, and El Greco and Jacopo da Pontormo were prominent Mannerist painters.

Minimalism

An art movement that developed in painting, sculpture and design in the 1960s. Rejecting the intense emotionalism and subjectivism of such movements as Abstract Expressionism, Minimalism sought an impersonal art, typically employing commercially produced, geometrical products (such as steel cubes) arranged in rows or series. Donald Judd, Carl André and Dan Flavin are among the most important artists of this movement. More generally, Minimalism describes forms of architecture or design that are stripped to bare essentials.

Obelisk

(Latin *obeliscus*, Greek *obelískos*: "pointed column") A four-sided, tapering stone column in the form of a very slender pyramid, used as a solitarily standing monument.

Orangerie

Originally, an exotic collection of citrus trees at European courts in the 16th century. In time, the term was used of the buildings or rooms used to protect the trees. Often elegantly designed, these were often used for social events.

Pantheon
(Greek *pan*: "all" and *theós*: "god")
In ancient Greece, a sanctuary dedicated
to "all the gods". Over time, this meaning
expanded and today the term is generally
used of a monument honouring a country's
illustrious dead. The oldest preserved
building of this kind is the Pantheon in Rome,
which was erected under Emperor Hadrian
in the 2nd century AD.

Pylon
In Ancient Egyptian architecture, a heavy,
tapering tower that forms part of the monumental gate leading to a temple complex.
In modern architecture, pylons are either
supporting or framing structures intended
to absorb compressive forces (eg the pylons
carrying electricity cables).

Relief
A sculpture in which the forms project from a
flat surface (of stone, wood, metal or ivory).
Reliefs were often used to decorate the sur-
faces of buildings, such as the walls (internal
and external), pediments and church portals.
They were particularly popular in ancient
Greece and Rome, and also Renaissance
Italy.

Spolia
(Latin *spolium*: "booty, something taken from
the enemy") Building elements plundered
from older buildings (especially those of
antiquity) in order to be reused in a later
building. Typically columns, sculptures,
friezes, capitals, architraves, lintels etc.
Originally, old buildings were exploited
simply because they provided an inexpensive
source of building material. In time, however,
the cultural references made by the spolia
became increasingly important.

Stupa
(Sanskrit *stup*: "pile up, accumulate")
Originally, a round mound of earth built up
over a grave. Within a few centuries, this
simple burial mound developed into the basic
form of the classical Buddhist stupa: a square
platform on which sits a hemispheric dome
surmounted by a crown and spire. The oldest
construction of this kind, found in Sanchi in
Central India, was built in the third century
BC.

Tracery
The ornate stone ribbing in the windows of
Gothic churches. Its basic purpose is struc-
tural – it supports large areas of glass – but
it also has an important decorative function.
It developed during the High Gothic era in
France and reached its peak in the English
Perpendicular Style.

Transept
In a church, one of the short "arms" that
intersects the nave at the east end, near
the altar, usually aligned north-south.

INDEX

PHOTO CREDITS